Aquarian Labyrinth

A New Pattern for a New Age

Llynnette VanHooser

Table of Contents

We are Circle, within circle
With no beginning, and never ending...

Thank You

The making of this book has had a lot of twists and turns, just like the labyrinth…
There were times when writing this book just seemed silly so I would shelf the project for a few months to a year, depending on how life was going at the time. Although it's not very long, it took a long time to allow things to unfold enough to have something to write about.
There were several people who took this journey with me and needless to say, it was not always an easy journey for them, to watch me not sure of what I was doing. To them, I would like to give special thanks!

Smiley - Thank you for the years of emotional support, support and service with all of my various crazy projects, inspiration and editing. You are amazing, I love you more than you can fathom!
Peter - Thank you for your willingness. If you had not said, "YES", to the first labyrinth build none of this would have happened. You have created majik! Blessings my friend! I love you!
Wilbur Hot Springs - Dr Richard L Miller and Jolee Miller - Thank you for allowing me to change the already beautiful landscape in the sanctuary! Thank you to all of the staff at Wilbur for embracing the labyrinth project! I love you!

Uncle Phil - Thank you for always being my cheering section, support & service and being one of my editors. I love you!

Maggie - I know you are always in my corner. Thank you for listening when needed and giving sound advice when solicited. I love you, my froggy friend!

Mel - Such a small name for such a person. Thank you for you love and support. You may not realize it, but you help more than you know! I love you!

Terrye - For always lending an ear and a hug. Thank you for your help with the editing. Love you sister!

To all of my wonderful friends and family, blessings, and be well!!

About the Author – Llynnette

Llynnette VanHooser, is a California Certified Massage Therapist, Reiki Master, Health Educator, Geomancer and Mystic. At this writing has more than 20 years massage and energy work experience.

Although she grew up in the San Francisco Bay area, she now resides in Clearlake, Ca, where she has a private practice, Aquarian Body Harmonics. She runs her business from her home that she shares with her life partner, Smiley as well as a menagerie of cats, dogs, chickens, ducks, goats and a big silly horse named Whiskey: aka WTF (Whiskey Tango Foxtrot). Living the dream in their incense scented, artistic and eclectic styled home.

Besides healing therapies, Llynnette multifaceted interests and has been involved in many endeavors along the way, always returning to her passion of healing therapies.

Some of her other activities have included but are not limited to: performing at local weekend Renaissance Faires as her favorite and popular character "Luna

Viscosity Fermentia Stumblebell" - AKA The Bubble
Fairy. As a bubble artist, she created non-plastic
Eco-friendly bubble wands which works better than any
plastic wand you ever used. Although The Bubble Fairy
had what some would call a successful career ahead of
her, Llynnette left the spotlight of fame and glory, lol, to
once again return to her love of healing therapy work.

Her home is a 2.4 acre parcel in Northern California that
lends itself well to her various interests. This property
came to her in a majickal way just around the same time
that the Aquarian Labyrinth patterns came to her. It is
her intention to devote a portion of her property to the
building and teaching of labyrinths, dancing and
drum-circles and various interests.

Websites:

- Llynnette.com - Keep up on all I have going on.
- AquarianLabyrinth.com - The Aquarian Labyrinth
  - A new pattern for a new age
- AquarianBodyHarmonics.com - Energy Work,
  Sound & Frequency Therapy
- BubbleFairy.com - Luna the Magical Bubble
  Fairy
- DuWackyDu.com - Du-Wacky-Du Homestead

Introduction

What this book is: This book is the story of my personal discovery of the Aquarian Labyrinth. It is a book that introduces something new yet ancient. It is a story that may stretch your perception of the labyrinth and what the traditional patterns have taught you. This is a sharing experience of what I have been shown, and what I have learned through the teaching that has come from walking with my friend the labyrinth and especially the discovery of the new yet ancient Aquarian Labyrinth.

It is basically the meandering ramblings of the inner workings of my mind, and what the labyrinth has placed there while discovering its twisting turning journey.

What this book is not: This book is not a labyrinth history book, nor is it a complete explanation of labyrinths as they are traditionally known. Many authors have covered the labyrinth subject in depth, and sufficiently enough that I do not feel it necessary to attempt such an undertaking as I am far less qualified on those subjects than the people who have walked before me. (No pun intended)

If you are new to labyrinths I suggest you read other books on labyrinths as well to get a more rounded perspective of the traditional labyrinths of

the ancient world. I don't consider this text a
suitable introduction to labyrinths. Authors such as
Sig Lonegren, Lauren Artress and Gayle West have
done a fantastic job of covering the introduction and
history of traditional labyrinths. I have no desire to
redo work that has already been done.

The reason for writing this book is to introduce you,
the reader/adventurer, to a new set of patterns
which I have discovered and invite you to explore.
As such, the majority of the subject matter will refer
to these discovered patterns which I call
Continuous Path Labyrinths, or Aquarian Labyrinth
patterns. Reference to other writings will be made
when necessary.

I believe these newly discovered patterns have
much to teach us. If we allow for that to manifest. I
have experienced many lessons personally. Some I
choose to share here, and some I chose to keep
private. I encourage you to not only explore the
examples I give within this writing, but also to go on
and explore the patterns for yourself, then you too
can choose to share your experiences or keep
them to yourself.

To further what this book is not... it is not a book of
world wide maps and locations, although reading
such material is fascinating, again, I have found the
coverage of this subject to be quite complete, so
complete in fact that I have nothing further to

contribute, other than a few personal labyrinth locations on Google Earth. If you are interested in Labyrinth sites – Worldwide, may I suggest, going to the Labyrinth Society Website and looking on the World Labyrinth Locator Map where people register their labyrinth locations.

This book was not written or conceived by a professional metaphysicist, geomancer, scientist or archeologist. This book was simply written by someone who believes, a new pattern has come to light. A pattern that may have been overlooked for a long time.

It is not a complete guide on how to set-up or walk a labyrinth. Especially not the "traditional" patterns. I have however, included a diagram of how to draw a Cretan labyrinth for those new to labyrinths, and for reference to the seed pattern and how changes to that seed pattern resulted in the Aquarian Labyrinth Patterns - ALP's

This book is not a way to convince you believe the way I do. It is however an invitation to examine what you do believe.

What I hope this book is: I hope this book is inspirational to those who read it, and to those who decide to allow the labyrinths of the world to teach and guide them.

I hope this book will open hearts, heal lives and change people for the better, by working with the labyrinth patterns within.

I continue to find something new to learn in the friend and teacher which I have come to know as the Aquarian Labyrinth. I hope you will too!

"Finding Love, Peace, Joy and Healing the heart..."

Chapter 1 – First Contact

I vividly remember my first encounter with a labyrinth, although it was well over 15 years ago. Other than the movie Labyrinth, which had the potential to be a great movie, and the Greek mythology of the Minotaur's labyrinth, which in both cases were actually mazes, I had never heard of nor had I ever seen a labyrinth, much less walked one.

I was living in the Rochester area of upstate New York. I had the opportunity to become acquainted with, and take monthly classes at the historical and magical Lilydale. For those who are not familiar with Lilydale, it is a unique closed community associated with the spiritualist church. How I arrived at this place in my life is a very long and convoluted story which I will not bore you with here.

I was on a spiritual quest, but how I began that journey derailed my entire life. Regardless of the past karmic burden I had brought upon myself, for which I later consciously worked through. I found myself going to monthly classes which were paid for by the generosity of a woman I had met, by chance, in Montana. She was the reason I was in New York. She had invited me to come live with and help her sort through her life after the passing of her husband. It was a warm and symbiotic relationship that lasted for a while, and it served a purpose for us both.

If you have never been to Lilydale, all I can tell you is that it's majickal, it's beautiful, and the psychic energy is intense to say the least. It is so majickal in feeling, that when I saw the movie Harry Potter the first time, I had the same feeling as when I would return to Lilydale. Driving through the front gate made me feel like truly arriving home, kind of like how Harry felt when he would return to Hogwarts.

It was at about the third or fourth monthly retreat when I met Sig Lonegren. The first part of his presentation in the morning was about dowsing. How to use a pendulum and dowsing rods as well as uses of dowsing.

I had never heard of dowsing before. Although I had been dowsing since I was 12 and didn't know other people did it, or that it had a name. My mother had given me a crystal necklace which I would take off my neck and hold by the silver chain and ask it questions. I shared this ability with a friend once, and when she got answers that she didn't like or that "scared" her, she didn't come over to my house anymore. I guess that's what happens when you have the reputation of being the creepy girl in school.

When I met Sig it was very serendipitous, at least for me. I had made a few cloth card bags in various colors, and I brought several with me that weekend. One of them was blue and I had painted a silver lightning bolt on it. At the time that I painted it, I didn't know why. It was not a symbol that I usually worked with at the time. When I met him, I had a feeling to give him the blue bag. I like to give small tokens to teachers on the path out of respect. I presented him with a choice of three bags. Red, green & Blue – he chose the blue. He then told me he had misplaced his bag before he come on this trip. He found the lightning bolt to be interesting, as this, he claimed, was one of his power symbols. I about fell over.

In the evening after dinner, Sig gave a presentation about labyrinths and crop circles. He did it as a slide-show presentation and most of his emphasis was on labyrinths. The first slide I saw of a Cretan labyrinth had me hooked. I liked his simple and straightforward way of teaching. When he explained that the Cretan is often called the goddess labyrinth, I got very excited, for it was only months before that I had been touched by the goddess and my heart has never been the same... in a good way. He also talked about a goddess or witch that stirred her cauldron in the pattern of the labyrinth. I believe it was Cerridwin, but it's hard to

romomber from so long ago. If I meet him again I
will ask him.

As the slide-show progressed, we were shown a
picture of the Chartres Labyrinth, which was built in
a cathedral in Chartres France, in the 13th century.

Upon my first viewing of it, I felt a strong connection
and I couldn't understand how easily this style of
pattern could be created. For I felt very intimidated
by it. Almost as though it were taunting me, to
come learn, and discover it's lessons and secrets.

Since I have always been working on my self
esteem, and doubting my abilities the whole time, I
did not see how I could copy it and make it look
anywhere near as perfect and beautiful as I saw the
Chartres.

Although I found it beautiful, mysterious and perfect
in form of appearance, or appearance of form,
however you want to look at it. I had a feeling as I
looked at it, that one thing was missing... a
continuing path from the center out.

He also talked about ley-lines and how most
labyrinths or ancient stone circles have been
placed on various important coordinates according
to some sacred geometric formula. Ley-lines were
a new concept for me, although somehow
instinctively I knew this. I started studying chakras

and meridians within the body just before this workshop so it all fit well together.

Two of the most important things I learned during that weekend was:

1 – How to draw a 7 circuit Cretan labyrinth, from what is known as a seed pattern

2- The difference between a maze and a labyrinth. A maze is a puzzle that can have multiple paths and even dead endings, where the path of the labyrinth is a walking meditation of a singular path,.

A maze is intended to confuse, and to be a puzzle that is solvable, or possibly unsolvable, depending on who made it and how difficult it is. A maze has dead-ends and sometimes loops that bring you right back to the start.

A labyrinth on the other hand, is a single path. It spirals and meanders it's way eventually to the center, or goal, where one can wait or meditate further. Traditionally you would then follow the same path out the same way you came in. I later found that the path can also continue, to an exit different than the one you came in on, but more on this later. The type of labyrinth I will be talking about in this text is not as common and we will be looking at in depth, as the main focus of this book. However, I have gotten ahead of myself.

All of the information from Sig that I have mentioned thus far was given in the time frame of one day. This was a lot for me to assimilate. That night I had trouble going to sleep. However, I still woke energized as I tend to do when I sleep at Lilydale.

The second day of workshops was supposed to be mostly outside. However, Mother nature had other ideas. Rain started in heavy around 11:30 am so we had to move the workshop indoors. Before we got wet, I had the opportunity to take my first walk on the labyrinth. For me this was perfect, as I tend to like rainy days.

As I stood in the autumn drizzle admiring the beauty and simplicity of the seven circuit labyrinth stretched out before me. All could think of, is how it lacked an exit path, but who was I to judge?

I wasn't doing it consciously, it was more like a passing thought. So despite it's flawed nature, for my arrogant part, I found myself standing at the entrance to a new experience.

I closed my eyes, took a deep breath as if getting ready to jump into water. Exhaled as I took my first step onto the path. Upon my exhalation I breathed the words - "Help me, to know you." As I walked along this path of meandering, I found myself feeling as if I was making a sacred journey. My mind drifted near and far but I found my thoughts consistently came back to the beauty of the spiral. The spiral of life, and spirals in nature.

Our DNA is made up of spirals. Spirals within spirals. In our everyday modern lives we rarely come across spirals. Modern man has made this live, flowing, spherical world that we were created to live in and on, into a dead, stagnant, square world, that HE has built. It made me question how tuned into the earth are we? How tuned in am I?, and before I knew it, I was at the center, asking myself, How did I get here?

I stayed in the center only a moment or two. Other students had begun their journey to the center and I didn't want to cause a bottleneck. Besides, I had been watching a big thunder cloud come over the valley and it looked like it was going to dump in about 10 minutes or less. Which was about how long it would take to walk back out and over to the hotel. As I felt the drop in temperature creep up my spine I knew it would be soon. I so wanted to stand in front of the fire in the hotel lobby right now.

As I made my final pass around the center and stepped back onto the path, I had an overwhelming feeling of gratitude. So much so, I choked on what were becoming tears. My heartbeat quickened and I began to praise and thank spirit for the gifts laid before me. I began to give thanks for all of the

things in my life no matter how big or small.
Thanksgiving for things as simple yet profound as
my very breath. The spiral continued in my mind
and moved around my heart. I could feel the
healing power move through my body, as if the
labyrinth path had entered me somehow. This
experience was much more profound than I had
ever anticipated. I walked away from the labyrinth
with the feeling that something ancient and sacred
had happened. Almost like a type of initiation. The
goddess had touched me yet again.

As I walked back to the hotel lobby, it began to rain.
I was already wet and cold from the early morning
drizzle., and now the actual rain had come.
Interesting how that scenario was so well timed.

I entered the lobby of the hotel and went straight to
the fireplace. I was standing there warming my
hands and drying my hat, when Sig walked in
equally wet. It had really started pouring after I
came in and now it was hailing. I guess that
thunder cloud I was watching was right on time. He
too made a beeline for the fireplace as did those
who filed in behind him; all seeking warmth and dry.

As I was standing in front of the fireplace I noticed
the painting that resided over it. It was what I would
call an "elder" He had a beard and long white hair.
He was standing in a very spiritual looking pose.
His left arm was bent at the elbow and a 45 degree

angle, which put his left hand directly over his heart, palm facing up, forefinger pointing, thumb and middle finger touching. His right arm was also bent at a 45 degree angle with the lower part of his arm and hand pointing upwards or skyward. His hand was in a pointing position with the index finger extended and pointing straight up, thumb and middle finger touching.

I saw this painting before, but I never really "saw" it. It was always just background. Now it was making it's presence known. I was intrigued. I stood in front of the painting and began to physically copy the pose. I stood in the same position, and stared into those eyes of compassion.

When I stared into them long enough, I felt complete unconditional love, for the first time in my life that I was conscious of. I basked in this moment.

I stood there for close to an hour. At one point he seemed to come to life which was needless to say a little unnerving for a moment, until I drifted back into basking in his eyes. This experience doesn't have anything to do with labyrinths, other than the lesson of working with an oracle. If you work with one long enough, you will begin to unlock some of its secrets as you ask. This was the first time I ever had an experience with an oracle that I knew of. However, it would not be the last. Although, this

painting took me by surprise, I later realized that
even the labyrinth is a type of oracle.

Because of the rain, which turned into an early
storm, most of the afternoon activities were
canceled for the day. We had a choice, we could go
for a walk around the grounds, but who wants to
walk in the rain, or we could find something to
amuse ourselves, or take a nap.

Some people were gathering together in one of the
rooms in the lobby to practice what I describe as
parlor tricks. I chose to go for a walk around the
grounds, rain or not. As I walked, I noticed the birds
and how a flock of them were flying in
semi-formation, and how when they would come
out of formation they would weave themselves into
a spiral as they regrouped. I noticed the leaves as
they danced and spiraled around each other on the
breeze. I also noticed how the beautiful rare swans
in the pond seemed to dance with one another as
they spiraled around each other in the water. Then I
found myself back in front of the labyrinth without
consciously looking for it. I sensed that our last
encounter was not yet finished. The rain had
stopped and the remains of the day broke through
the clouds to shine rays down from on high. Then
suddenly and just for a moment a rainbow shone
over the pond. I have no other words to say, except
picturesque, peaceful, perfect. To this day, when I
need to find my "happy place", I return to that

particular moment. Some people have to create their happy place, I feel blessed in that I have actually been there.

So there I stood at the mouth of the labyrinth, looking fondly upon it like an old friend even though we had just met. This time I did not notice the "errancy" of it not having an exit. All the physical had passed away and only what was important remained. This time no one was around so I felt at liberty to take my time. I looked down at my feet as I stood again at the threshold of the labyrinth. Noticing how the basic design resembles the goddess - Arms stretched out, hair flowing, free form, graceful, captivating. It was as if an ancient time was reaching out to me, waiting for me to take the hand of the ancestors. As before, I took a deep breath, closed my eyes and exhaled, as I took my first step. In the same moment I exhaled, I again said, " help me, to know you." I walked the path this time with much expectation and little hesitation. I found myself anticipating unlocking all of the wonders of this new found tool. I meandered slowly, waiting for it to speak to me again as it did before. As I walked I started to get a feeling of disappointment. The feeling grew as I found my way to the center. Nothing profound happened... no visions, no messages, no lightning bolts, just a big nothing. At this point I was truly disappointed. Why had I gotten something last time and nothing this time? What did I do wrong? What did I do last time that I didn't' do this time? My good ole' ego and self talk kicked in and my mind was full of questions as to why...

As I stood there feeling defeated, I quieted my heart enough to hear two little words... "Thank You". It was at this moment I had the amazing revelation I was looking for. I remembered how in my last walk I was giving thanks as I left the center and was on my way back out. I had received this same thing last time also but it took me until now to get it all together in my mind. I'm just a little slow sometimes. The lighting bolt that hit me was this, Are you going to be thankful only when you receive something, or are you going to be grateful at all times?

I continued on my path as I gave thanks for receiving, and most of all for not receiving, for just being.

Although my heart was full of gratitude for what I had received, I still wanted more. As the day drew to a close and the sun set, I thought. My lessons were over for the day. Much to my joyful surprise, it wasn't, and I am thankful!

Chapter 2 - A Little Song and Dance

Dancing the Labyrinth Path, Songs & Chants

After dinner, the facilitators of the workshops made a small auditorium available to Sig as it was starting to get very cold outside and by now was quite dark. Sig got everyone together for some team building exercises with the class. Some of them I remember from camp fire girls, gee who even remembers those? One of the games he did involved 4 bricks and 2 boards, where the whole class was on one big team. The object is to get everyone across the "river of acid" and each person can only cross once. I don't know the actual name of the activity but it is a very good team builder!

The activity that impressed me the most was a "dance" that he taught us. We were inside the auditorium with the storm outside gearing up for snow. I could feel the energy grow as the dance began. First he taught us a simple chant. The tune is very old. I have heard many versions of the lyrics to the same tune, but I had never heard of this one. The version I was most familiar with was Rose Red. If you ever spent any time at Renaissance Faire,

I'm sure you've heard it. It's most beautiful when sung in a round with three. The song I heard that night was also sung in such a round.

The version I heard that night was. Dear friends, dear friends – will I ever see thee again- you have given me your treasure- I love you so.

We sung it in a round that night, and the ancient power was thick in the air. Not only did we sing this song, but we also danced a very simple dance that was more like walking in rhythm than dancing. We held hands starting in a circle and ending up in a spiral. As this spiral continued, I could feel the majickal/psychic energy building in the room.

Once the first person in the chain reached the center, they would go under the arms of the people that were in front of them working their way back out of the spiral. It was at this time that the energy started to subside. It was also at this time that the thought came to me again. A continuous path would make it possible to do a dance like this. I really didn't give it much more thought than, Gee that would be nice if...

I have since learned that power is built on such fleeting thoughts. Sometimes your subconscious for whatever reason will decide to hold on to something like that and run with it, unbeknownst to us.

15 years later...

Shortly after the new pattern came to me, I started hearing a tune in my head. This is nothing new for me, as I usually have a tune or two running around in my head. What was odd about this tune is that I hadn't heard it in quite a while. It's not usually a song a sing. It was a tune that is usually sung in a round with at least two other people, as I had mentioned earlier in this chapter, and I didn't have any singing partners at the time.

This tune coming to mind started me thinking about that night so long ago in Lilydale. The trouble was, at the time I couldn't remember the words to it. I remembered how it felt to hold hands in a group and dance in a spiral. It flashed in my head and in my heart. I realized that a dance of this sort could be done on the new labyrinth pattern. Since this pattern has both an entrance and an exit that are right next to each other – a group could start a the beginning and dance all the way through the labyrinth then go right back in to start again since no one has to give room to pass for people coming out. I knew instinctively the flow would be amazing, and I longed for the time when I could experience that flow. Suddenly I had an image of just that. A group of people dancing the labyrinth. Raising the awareness of peace and healing. Not just for the planet collectively, but for each of us individually.

Indigenous cultures of all continents have used
dance as part of their spiritual walk. As part of their
healing, and as part of their majick. I believe that
every-time we walk a labyrinth, the planet heals a
little more. The more labyrinths that are built and
used, the more healing occurs. Not only for the
plant but for her people as well. Each step on the
labyrinth path is a step towards peace. I will talk
more about that later.

I could see people singing and dancing the
labyrinth, turning and dancing, singing and
weaving. I thought about it all day as if another
riddle had been placed before me to solve. The
labyrinth is a riddle in and of itself, and now it was
asking me to find It's song. The tune was there, it
just needed words.

Months later as I was building the first Aquarian
Labyrinth, the words came to me, while I was down
on my knees placing stones. With the tune still
playing in my head, the words came to me in such
a flood, I had to run to my car to get a pen and
paper. I am not a wordsmith by any means. I am
not one who is known for writing songs or poetry.
On the contrary, these gifts usually evade me. So
the idea that this even happened was just one more
amazing experience to add to the long list of
amazing circumstances on this wonderfully special
journey I now found myself on.

As I said before, the words just came in a rush, and those words were: Labyrinth, Labyrinth - Walk this spiral path of light - Finding Peace, Love, Joy and Healing - At the heart.

This was such an overwhelming experience for me because as I said before, I am not usually lyrical. After that day the tune was there, in my head, every day until the labyrinth was complete, and then some.

On the day we consecrated the labyrinth which happened to be Winter Solstice 2011, I walked it and sang the song as I walked. It was wonderful. It set a nice pace for walking. I had to watch my footing periodically where the rocks were a little close together, But still the pace was perfect for strolling through the twists and turns in rhythm. I could feel the energy grow as I made the last few rounds before the path goes to the center. When I reached the center, I could feel a playfulness, and a definite healing vibration permeated the atmosphere. Besides the incense and sage that was burning, I could see a light mist that seemed to envelop the area of the labyrinth.

The air was still and created a kind of smokey bubble around the labyrinth, but it wasn't really smoke, it was something else. More like a type of spirit cloud, where the spirit gets so thick over an area that it will appear smokey or misty.

The song permeated my dreams for weeks, at times accompanied by dancers. I wasn't sure why this was. I was actually confused by it. Then I realized that I knew all along. We are sentient beings, meaning that we have senses, five to be exact, and the music/singing/dancing was stimulating a different portion of my senses by adding dancing, rhythm, a heartbeat. My heartbeat, the earth's heartbeat, humanity's heartbeat. As the last line of the song says, "...at the heart", which can also be sung as "...in my heart". The heartbeat of the labyrinth is an extension of our collective heartbeat as a race. What if the labyrinth were a key to unlocking how to realign our hear with the heart of our Earth Mother – Mother Earth?

Being a body-worker, I notice a big difference in the way my clients relax depending upon if have music playing in the background opposed to when I don't. I notice when there isn't music, they seem to want to fill in the silence with something so they tend to get chatty and that usually distracts from full relaxation.

I know how important the senses are. Because I do bodywork I try to incorporate the five scenes as much as possible into what ever modality I am working in. I believe it opens the client up to a deeper experience, and gives them a chance to possibly connect with their sixth sense and be much more proactive in their healing experience.

I believe the same to be true with the labyrinth. It has the ability to engage all of our senses if we allow it.

After the first labyrinth was finished, I found myself singing and sometimes humming the labyrinth song. After a while I also found myself dancing. Not dancing in the conventional or modern sense, but dancing in an ancient sense.

This felt old, both in it's rhythm and in its simplicity. If you are a dancer you may find it a bit boring. However ,if you are allowing spirit to guide the dance, you will find it easy to follow, and the flow that happens will soon show you that there is more to dancing the labyrinth than what appears on the surface.

Basically it's just walking in rhythm. One foot in front of the other to the rhythm of the music or even the sacred rhythm of your heart. It can be done by just dancing through the labyrinth, Or it can be done in other ways. My favorite is to turn sideways facing the center and continuing to face the center as the switchbacks try to turn me around the other way.

Another fun way to do it is like described above but without continually turning to the center and allowing yourself to be turned either toward the center or toward the outer circle by the switchbacks of the labyrinths turns. What will happen is this, you will sometimes be facing the people in front of you and sometimes they will have their back to you. Sometimes you will be moving in the same direction as the person you are facing and sometimes you will be traveling in the opposite direction. This makes another great metaphor for life, sometimes you are traveling in the same direction as those around you and sometimes you are traveling in a different direction than those around you, either way it's okay, we will all end up where we belong. This is one of the many lessons of the labyrinth. Everyone will walk it differently, in their own unique and beautiful way and none of them are wrong.

I see a dance

Since these labyrinth patterns are a continuous path labyrinth, I can see a dance of people; holding hands as they walk/dance the labyrinth. All of them snaking through the twists and turns of the path all the while singing a beautifully haunting three part round of the Labyrinth Chant.

Within a few rounds, the first person will reach the heart, at which point, everyone drops hands and gets quiet. Each one shifting from a collective meditative state to an individual meditative state, which actually brings us back to the collective.

Since this labyrinth pattern has a continuous path that does not require a u-turn at the heart/goal, it is possible to go right back in once reaching the end of the path. Each person can walk the labyrinth as many times as they need to until they feel they have reached an answer or conclusion to their particular question or situation. Some people will only walk it one time after changing to singular mode, while others may walk it several times before they feel they are "done".

The group chant and dance is an energy builder and helps to raise the psychic energy collectively which in turn makes it easier for us as individuals to tap into that energy. It helps us process the higher vibration quicker therefore intuitively finding an answer to the question we are asking or problem we are seeking an answer to.

Importance of energetic protection

It is very important that you surround yourself in a bubble of protection before you start any psychic activity. Especially when you are working in a group. You never know what kind of energy are being brought in by others, so it's just best to protect yourself!

Individual experiences

Everyone will have a different experience on their walk. Some may cry due to a long awaited breakthrough. While others may laugh for reasons only they can comprehend. Some will walk fast and some will walk slow. Just as our life walk is different for each person, so is this walk called the labyrinth. You may walk the labyrinth asking the same question over and over for a while, sometimes a year of more, or you may get answers right away. There is no wrong way to walk it. Listen to your intuition, follow your heart. If you are not used to using your intuition or following your heart, walk the labyrinth more frequently and it will come to you.

Dance your heart

Dancing the labyrinth may feel strange at first. The more you do it, the more natural it will become to you. If you like drumming or if you have always wanted to drum, this may be a good time to learn. Learn native songs and chants that mean something to you. You can do these activities on your own or maybe have a monthly moon dance where you can invite friends to come experience the fullness of the labyrinth.

I encourage you to get to know this aspect of the labyrinth as it has a type of freedom that comes with singing and dancing.

If you are not one who likes to dance maybe just slow your regular walking rhythm of your heart. Experiment, listen to your heart, listen to the labyrinth. Learning starts with exploration.

Take the time to learn to dance of your hearts song.

Songs & Chants

Labyrinth Song

Llynnette VanHooser - 2011

Labyrinth, Labyrinth

Walk this spiral path of light

Finding Peace, Love, Joy and Healing

At the heart

Sacred Grove

Llynnette VanHooser - 2012

Come with me to the sacred grove

as we work our rite, by the dark of night,

Come with me to the sacred grove

and we'll work our majik together.

Come with me to the sacred grove

as we work our rite, by the waxing light,

Come with me to the sacred grove

and we'll work our majick together.

Come with me into the forest

come with me to the sacred grove

singing, dancing, feasting, casting

majick is afoot in the sacred grove

Come with me to the sacred grove

as we work our rite, by the full moon light,

Come with me to the sacred grove

and we'll dance the labyrinth together.

Come with me to the sacred grove

As we work our rite, by the waning light,

Come with me to the sacred grove

And we'll work our majick together.

Come with me into the forest

come with me to the sacred grove

singing, dancing, making merry

Goddess is alive in the sacred grove

Elemental Chant

Llynnette VanHooser - 2012-2019

A: Wind blows, Fire glows,

Water flows, all around the Earth

B: Bless the Wind, breath of Mother

Bless the Fire, Spirit of Mother

Bless the Water, Lifeflow of Mother

Bless the Earth, her body.

Chapter 3 – A New Pattern

June of 2011 met me with a big life upheaval. Sometimes, stuff just happens. I ended up moving to Clearlake Ca from San Jose Ca. Geographically only about 150 miles, Culture wise - Millions of miles. I always knew I wanted to move to northern California, I just never took the time to decide on where. I just figured I'd do it later. I was too busy living in the city, which had grown up around me, and trying to figure out how to live in such a place. Once we moved, the slower pace took a little adjustment but was much needed and appreciated.

What is it they say, where one door closes God opens a window?! Well that's the only way I can describe how June of 2011 was for my husband and I. From the time we made the decision to go to Clearlake, everything just fell into place. Our call to Clearlake was two fold. One, family issues that had been brewing for years finally came to a head and I knew it was time to separate myself before it escalated any further. Two, a very good friend of my husband and I were living in Clearlake and needed our help. He was ill and had no one to help him. So at his word, off to Clearlake we went.

Clearlake is a majickal place! Allow me to describe the scenery of the area to you. First the lake elevation is at 1325 feet. We have mountains all the way around us, which to me makes it seem like a giant cauldron. Then there is a mountain, beautiful majestic Konocti. She is actually a volcano and there is a symbiotic relationship between the mountain and the lake. The lake is mostly spring fed all year long and is not very deep, only 38 feet at the deepest. I have been around the country and lived in such beautiful places as Oregon, Montana, upstate New York and Tennessee. I have been to other beautiful places in northern California, such at Shasta, and many other places on the coast, but when I arrived at Clearlake I truly felt, not only was I called here, I was finally home. The more I study the area and the more I look at and spend time with Konocti, the more I see that I am where I need to be, and it's wonderful!

The city of Clearlake has some cultural issues and the lake itself has some ecological issues. It's very hot in the summer, sometimes weeks of over 100 degree weather. Then months of hovering around 32 in the winter and it rarely snows, but even with all that, I still would rather live here than where I grew up. I have always considered myself a wildflower so wherever I am planted I do my best to bloom. Sometimes you have to look at where you are and just say be grateful!

So here I was in Clearlake, knew no-one but our friend, was on unemployment and now living in a financially depressed area. On the outside things looked pretty bleak. But on the inside things were bubbling and churning. My dream was becoming vivid and the whole time I had the feeling of being carried on angels wings, is the only way I can describe it.

San Jose was left behind in kind of a hurry. Usually I was living hand to mouth and the thought of moving was a task that would normally seem insurmountable. However, somehow we had the money, the time and the people to help us all in perfect timing. Obviously Spirit had planned it because I could not have planned it any better. The feeling of being carried started when we made the decision to move and continued until several months after we landed in Clearlake.

If you have ever experienced this you will know what I mean. I know I am not the only one this has ever happened to. This also was not the first time this had happened to me. It was fantastic, scary, reassuring and confusing all at the same time, but mostly it was wonderful! On one hand I felt empowered yet on the other hand I felt moved, like a piece on a chess board.

At times of stress I tend to draw, or more like doodle. Through the years drawing labyrinths has become a sort of meditation for me. When I get stressed or am thinking a lot, I tend to draw labyrinths over and over again. Then I sit and run it with my fingor. I find this exercise to be not only meditative but mentally therapeutic in that the mind seems to go into problem solving mode when running the labyrinth either with the finger or for those who are lucky enough to have access to one that can be walked regularly.

After the move, I started drawing labyrinths and doodling again. I was also taking long walks and meditating a lot more than I had been in a while. I have found meditation very beneficial in the past. I find it to be very effective with self healing and to overcome hurt emotions. Sometimes drawing can cause me to go into a type of trance or meditative state, to where I do a lot of problem solving that I would not usually be able to do. Personally I believe it to be my higher self showing me the easier way to do things. Once I get out of the way and let the process happen it's a beautiful thing.

One day while drawing a seed pattern I started playing with the dynamics of the seed pattern layout. I moved some corners and dots around so that there was not an even number going around the cross in the middle. (You may understand what I mean later when you read about seed patterns.) I didn't really give it much thought, I just started drawing the connecting lines and suddenly when I got the last circuit, there it was in all its glory. A six circuit labyrinth that on first inspection looks deceptively like a Cretan labyrinth, but in fact was something quite different.

I just sat there and stared at it for a long time. Almost afraid to move or tell anyone for fear that it might be a dream or that it wasn't real. The idea started soaking in that I had discovered a new pattern without trying. I immediately started to cry as the feelings of gratitude and thanksgiving overwhelmed me. I felt like I had been blessed to discover such a jewel, such a treasure. I felt like I had just unraveled an ancient riddle.

For days I just went around drawing it over and over again, thinking somehow it was going to change, but it didn't. I realized it had chosen me and the thought made me both giddy and terrified! The whole time in the back of my mind I could hear this little voice saying,"Build it". Build it?! Are you crazy? I just moved here, I don't really know anyone. My life has just gone through upheaval. I don't have any property to put it on. What do you mean build it? I guess hearing a little voice may sound strange to some people, and then to answer it might just make me crazy. Well my sanity has never been a point of contention with most people who know me. I have heard that same small voice most of my life and I have learned to trust it. Even though sometimes the circumstances may not seem good in the beginning it always works out to be good in the end. I just have to hold on to learning from the present experience. Circumstances change, and if I listen they will usually change for the better. So I listened. More on that later.

As I continued to draw the pattern over and over, I also started to expand the same pattern and found that if I added one extra corner all the way around the seed pattern I would get different size labyrinths and they all worked. Meaning they all made a complete path that had a starting point, a goal and an ending point.

I increased the original pattern by one corner and then connected the dots just like usual. The original pattern has 6 circuits. An increase of the original seed pattern by one makes it 10 circuits. An increase of two makes it 14 circuits. Originally I had only these three patterns. The first Aquarian Labyrinth that I laid out, is 14 circuits, it lives in Clearlake and has a beautiful view of Konocti, the magical,dormant volcanic mountain that overlooks the Clearlake area. But it wasn't long before I started playing with the size again. I decreased the pattern by one and created a simple 2 circuit labyrinth.

I also increased it one more time from my previous largest, bringing the total up to 18 circuits. What is so interesting about this pattern is that the path from the entrance to the goal is 10 circuits, and from the goal to the exit is 8 circuits.

Upon discovery of the 18 circuit pattern, after adding what I call switchbacks to the outer portion, I noticed a similarity of both the Chartres and the Cretan in one labyrinth. This again was just another happy accident, it just came out that way. All I was doing was moving dots and corners around on a page then playing connect the dots. After the first one appeared on paper, as I realized what I had, I just sat there and stared at it for the longest time, not sure what to think.

I knew I wanted to lay this one out! Every time I ran this new pattern with my finger on paper, I could just imagine the energy that would be created from this magical earthwork. It is truly an amazing piece of work and at this writing I am collecting rocks to create this mammoth on my property in Clearlake.

I have looked at many labyrinths over the past 20 years. I have ran them on paper with my finger, I have walked them in person, But it wasn't until the discovery of these patterns, that I truly felt excited about physically building one.

Labyrinth Components and Language

If you are not already familiar with labyrinths I have added this section so you can understand what I am talking about as I explain different aspects of the labyrinth. Following is a brief explanation of the various components which make up the Labyrinth.

Seed Pattern = A visual formula for drawing or laying out a labyrinth.

Circuit = A labyrinth path, pertaining to one full round or ring of the labyrinth.

Heart/Goal = The center of the labyrinth. Traditionally the center is called the goal. In the case of the Aquarian Labyrinth Patterns, the center is called the heart. Although the whole labyrinth walk is a meditation, the heart is a place of stilling the self and reflecting, it can also be a place of great illumination.

Path = The portion of the labyrinth that is walked upon.

Wall = The lines that delineate or mark the space between the paths. Traditionally made from stone or earth but can be wood, rope, chalk, paint, etc.

Where did these Aquarian Labyrinth Patterns come from?

It's easy to look at these patterns and think that I sat down and spent many hours trying to figure out how to make something new. However, as much as I would like to take credit for being a super genius, it would not be true. I didn't' spend hours and days trying to unlock this puzzle. Instead it was instantaneous. Once I changed the seed pattern everything else fell into place and all the other patterns that came out of it were just as amazing. Did I create something new, or did I discover something that was there all along?

Personally I don't feel that I created it, I feel that I discovered it. That is was there all along. This is the reason I originally called them Faerie Labyrinths. It was as if the Faeries had guided me to find some small bit of ancient knowledge. Being a faerie myself, or so some believe, I feel privileged to share this with the mortals.

I have seen only one other labyrinth that almost looks like someone was trying to make the same pattern I discovered. Sig Lonegren talks about it in his book, Labyrinths, Ancient Myths and Modern Uses, pg 24.

Apparently it was created by the Hopi's and there are 4 different patterns that have been found in the area. One of them is a square labyrinth that has two paths at the entrance. This is the only similarity that the pattern has to the Aquarian patterns.

When I first saw this Hopi pattern my heart skipped a beat, as I thought it was the same as the revealed pattern but on closer examination I found that it was actually two paths that meander and then end within the labyrinth separately. There is not a goal to the pattern in the traditional sense. There is simply two completely separate paths in one labyrinth starting and ending at different points. It is looked at by the Hopi as an emulation of Mother and unborn child. Basically there are two labyrinths in one. The inner and the outer. The inner labyrinth takes the left path while the outer labyrinth takes the right path. One nesting inside the other. It is a great way to look at this beautiful symbol of mother and child.

Upon studying this pattern I realized that the changes that I made to the classic seed pattern were very similar to the changes that would have been made to this Hopi pattern. The only thing difference in the seed patterns, was the dot on the top right quadrant was missing in the Hopi pattern.

After looking at the seed pattern, and realizing the difference, I now was not sure if I had rediscovered something or if I had discovered it for the first time. My higher mind seemed to look into the past and think about those people so long ago who made a similar discovery. I could feel the ancestors reaching out to me, sharing with me knowledge, and vision.

So where did they come from? The only answer I have is, I'm not sure... maybe it was the faeries...

What is so special about this pattern?

I would not say this pattern is any better or more special than any other pattern ancient or modern. I find it to be so completely different from any pattern I have encountered in the past that I can't help but fly its flag and get it recognized in the labyrinth community.

These patterns are not better than a traditional pattern, they are just different. I believe all labyrinth patterns have a purpose. At the time of this writing, I believe this is a dancing labyrinth. I believe this pattern can aid us in our personal and collective healing for the planet. Just as walking a traditional labyrinth path is or can be a walk of peace. I believe this pattern to be a "Dance of Peace".

What makes this pattern and the others that came from the expanded and contracted seed patterns, completely unique from all others is the simple fact that the path goes to the goal and then the path continues to the exit. How? Why? I'm not sure, that's just how it came out.

Some may say that there are already patterns that do this. I would have to agree, however, on those that DO exit on a continuous path, the exit path is a straight one, almost like an escape route.

In the case of the Aquarian Labyrinth, the "exit" path is meandering like the rest of the labyrinth. It is very much a labyrinth within a labyrinth. As the outer labyrinth expands and contracts in size and number of circuits the inner labyrinth also expands and contracts.

I feel one of the main functions of this series of patterns is dancing and ceremonies as I mentioned earlier. Also the way these patterns are setup with an exit path, I believe it is for healing. The idea that once a person is healed from something, there is no need to go back over the same ground. Once the goal is visited we are changed therefore we are now free to walk a new path.

The exit path is the path of gratitude. Just as the entrance is a path of love. The two highest vibrations in the universe.

What does it look like?

I'm sure at this point I have talked way too much and you are wanting to see for yourself what I am talking about.

Placing the 6 circuit Aquarian labyrinth and a classic 7 circuit "Cretan" labyrinth side by side, right away, you can see their similarities and their differences. The six circuit Aquarian Labyrinth is the smallest of the Aquarian Labyrinth series.

Classical: 7 circuit "Cretan" Labyrinth.

Mew Age: 6 Circuit "Aquarian" Labyrinth

The first thing you may notice is how much they resemble each other in their basic shape and the "goddess" in the center is still very prominent. In the larger versions the goddess looks more balanced. However, it is still possible to see her outstretched arms just as with the "Cretan".

Then notice that instead of one path at the opening there are two. Intuitively people seem to gravitate to the one on the left. Either path will take you to the goal, however, I do believe that walking it from left to right creates and builds more energy than walking it from right to left. - Keep in mind I am still discovering.

I suggest you run each of these labyrinths with your finger or a stylus, just as if you were walking it, to get the feel of the energy that is created. Do you feel a difference between the two patterns? Did you remain in the goal of one or the other longer? Did you feel, hear, see anything?

Now look at the two patterns and concentrate on the paths themselves. Notice that they are almost identical in how many times the path turns and when. It's very interesting how similar they are to each other, but yet how very different.

Notice how the path meanders similar to the classic 7 circuit "Cretan", with one big difference, it only takes 4 circuits to reach the goal with the Aquarian, then once leaving the goal, it takes 2 circuits to reach the Exit.

When I first discovered this I was amazed at how easy it was to create despite its appearance. Although the above pattern was the first breakthrough pattern I discovered, there were more to come and each one has a different energy. Not good not bad, just different. I am still in the process of studying each of them for any hidden mysteries I may glean out of them, and I'm sure it will be a lifelong endeavor that I very much look forward to.

I sometimes feel like an explorer or archeologist, It's hard for me to imagine that this pattern has been overlooked for so long Or maybe it was just left for someone else to discover. Or maybe I'm just making too much out of the whole thing. Who knows?!

I hope that this pattern will quicken your pulse and inspire new found enthusiasm for a new type of labyrinth pattern. Those that have walked these patterns introduced in this book, and are familiar with labyrinths, usually tell me they like how the flow of these labyrinths feel. I am not saying one is better than the other, I'm merely passing on what others have shared with me.

As you move forward, I ask that you do so with an open mind and an open heart. I truly believe these patterns have been brought to us at this time for a purpose. For healing both ourselves and the planet, for deeper inner connection to ourselves and the planet, for building insight and intuition as well as inner journeying. I believe that dancing the labyrinth will bring a new found appreciation for ancient teachings, open us up for learning and help us to tune into the ancient heartbeat of our mother. The question is... are we willing to work and listen?

Chapter 4 – Seed Patterns: Then and now

This chapter will talk about seed patterns. Their purpose and how to make them how to use them, and the differences between the classic labyrinth seed pattern and the Aquarian labyrinth seed pattern. We will be focusing mostly on the Aquarian pattern in this chapter as it is the true subject of this writing.

Drawing a 7 circuit "Cretan" labyrinth

The above illustration shows how to draw a simple classical 7 circuit labyrinth. I will not go into detail here as it is well covered in other texts. I first learned how to do this from Sig Lonegren in the workshop I talked about earlier. This basic pattern creates a 7 circuit labyrinth and is the basis of all other classic labyrinths, including one of the most famous, The Chartres Labyrinth in France.

As I mentioned earlier, I did not say to myself, "I think I'll make a new labyrinth pattern." I simply discovered it, kinda by accident and then after playing around with what I had discovered, I found several more patterns that emerged as easily as the first.

While looking at the classic seed pattern on a piece of paper one day. I started thinking about a pattern I saw a few days before. It was a seed pattern that was in a Y shape, instead of a cross. I noticed that the "L's" were of a different number above the "Y" as it was below the Y. When this seed pattern was "invoked" by drawing the circuits in the standard way, It made a short 3 circuit continuous path labyrinth. This fascinated me, so one day I applied that same principle to the cross seed pattern. Once I moved some L's and dots around in a playful kind of way. I made a basic pattern. Cross in the middle, one L and one dot in the bottom left quadrant, one L and one dot in the top left quadrant, then I did something a little different. I place just a dot in the top right quadrant, and moved the missing L to the bottom right quadrant. It was that simple. Move one L and one dot, and a whole new pattern emerged.

There was one change made to starting this seed pattern. On a classic seed pattern you start at the center and move to the left or right, depending on the direction you want the pattern to go, making a loop that ends at the top of the first L in the direction you are going. When I drew the walls, as I was used to doing, it did not make a labyrinth. It just made paths and not all of them connected.

The next time I drew it I connected the top of the L in the left quadrant, skipped over the center cross-top and joined my first loop to the top of the dot in the right quadrant. Continuing the pattern just as if I was drawing a Cretan, following the new flow, I could see the pattern emerging. Once I finished drawing the last wall on the outside, I just sat there looking at it. It looked like all the elements were there, with an added one. The first thing I noticed was the two paths at the opening. Every other labyrinth I had seen, only had one path. Then I ran the pattern with my finger and found that the path was indeed continuous. It meandered all the way to the goal with no problem, but to my surprise, it then continued on, with two more circuits before it created an exit to the right of the mouth. It was better than something I could purposefully create or imagine.

I was astonished!! It took a few moments for it to soak in. I thought for a moment, it must be a mistake. So I drew another one, with the same result. What is it Einstein said? "The definition of insanity is doing the same thing over and over expecting a different result." That's just what I did too, drawing it over and over, thinking something was going to change. Until it finally soaked in that I just might have discovered something quite different. This realization brought much gratitude and thanksgiving in my heart and my spirit soared like a hawk!

Drawing a 6 circuit Aquarian Labyrinth

In this section I will explain how to draw the first pattern I discovered in this series. It is important to draw labyrinths as well as walk them. When you walk them you experience what is already there. When you draw one or lay one out you are experiencing what is not there, and bringing it to reality. Birthing it so to speak. So get a piece of paper and a pencil to draw the patterns I will be talking to you though. If you are looking to walk the sacred path, knowing how to create it makes it much more intimate. The various patterns have different energies and each one is like an old friend. As you draw these patterns, pay attention to these energies while your are drawing, and while you are "running" the patterns with your finger or pencil. Keep an open mind and an open heart and together we can explore the mysteries within this new yet ancient mystical tool. I believe that drawing labyrinths brings a deeper feeling of connection with the labyrinth.

AL Seed Pattern Exercise

At this point, I am guessing that you have already drawn a classic pattern from the seed pattern on the previous pages. If you are new to Labyrinths, I recommend you draw a classic labyrinth at least once before moving on the following exercise. If you are not new to labyrinth and have drawn them before, please move on to the next exercise.

On a piece of paper draw the following seed pattern as shown in the following illustration. I will try to explain it here. Start with a small even tinned cross. In the top left quadrant draw an L shape emulating the cross in that quadrant, and one dot evenly spaced from the L. In the top right quadrant make a dot evenly spaced from the cross. In the bottom right quadrant draw two L shapes emulating the cross in that quadrant evenly spaced from each other, and one dot evenly spaced from the second L. In the bottom left quadrant, draw an L shape emulating the cross in that quadrant, and one dot evenly spaced from the L just like the one in the top left.

If my instructions are not clear, just look at the picture I have drawn for you and copy it by following the arrows. You may even want to make photo copies of this seed pattern to draw on until you get a feel for laying it out.

Once you have a seed pattern, lay the paper in front of you and set the point of your pencil on the very top of the L in the top left quadrant, and draw an arch over the top of the cross ending at the dot in the top right quadrant. You have now made the goal. With practice you can make the goal more bulbous to make it look more like the goddesses head. It will require adjusting the other circuits as you go of course. For now, just do a simple arch.

- Place the tip of your pencil on the dot in the top left quadrant. Draw an arch, following the curve of the last "wall" you drew, ending at the end of the cross arm that is pointing to the right. You have now made the first circuit.
- Place the tip of your pencil on the end of the L that is pointing to the left in the top left quadrant. Draw an arch, following the curve of the last "wall" you drew, ending in the bottom right quadrant at the first L that is pointing to the right. You have now made the second circuit.
- Place the tip of your pencil at the end of the left side cross arm. Draw an arch ending in the bottom right quadrant to the second L that is pointing to the right. You have now made the third circuit.
- Beginning in the bottom left quadrant at the end of the L where it points to the left. Draw

an arch, following the curve of the last "wall"
you drew, ending in the bottom right
quadrant at the dot. You have now made
the fourth circuit. By now this should start to
feel very intuitive. If you already draw
labyrinths this should feel familiar.

- Starting in the bottom left quadrant at the
  dot. Draw an arch ending in the bottom right
  quadrant where the second L points down.
  You have now made the fifth circuit.
- Starting in the bottom left quadrant at the
  end of the down pointing L. Draw an arch,
  ending in the bottom right quadrant where
  the first L points down. You have now made
  the sixth and final circuit.

Switchbacks

In my study of labyrinths over the past twenty something years, one of the most interesting discoveries of building with more circuits comes from how the paths respond to the addition of u-turns or what I call switchbacks. Chartres is a perfect example of that. The pattern is no more than an 11 circuit classic made into a circle, with the addition of switchbacks. When adding switchbacks some of the paths may have to be minimally adjusted as they come down to meet the entrance. These adjustments are simple and relatively intuitive.

Any of the patterns I will be revealing in this writing can be used either with or without switchbacks, and they can be made in the classic organic style, round, square or octagonal. Of course, changing them from the original organic pattern will take a little work on your part to figure out... but that's half the fun!

I would like to add here one more interesting difference in the layout of the switchbacks in the classic patterns and the Aquarian patterns. In the classic patterns like Chartres, the switchbacks are placed at varying places that are not even on the wheel if you were to look at it just as a visual element, it is something that makes it seem off balance in a way. However after examining it you will discover it was the only way it could be done for it to come out in the pattern it creates.

When I added switchbacks to the Aquarian patterns I tried to add the switchbacks at these same varying places as the Chartres but the path would get lost every time. It wasn't until I "balanced" them that they worked. When I say balanced I mean, if there is a switchback on the left or west side that skips the first circuit and lands in the second and third from the edge. Then the opposite side, right or east, should be the same. Then the top would be offset by one. In this example that would mean the switchback, at the top/west side, would fall in the first circuit. The reason for this, is all the classic patterns are odd numbered and all the Aquarian patterns are even numbered.

I had never seen anyone besides myself use switchbacks on a 7 or in my case a 6 circuit labyrinth, until I visited the First Unitarian Church in my hometown of San Jose, CA.

After a fire gutted the sanctuary of the First Unitarian Church in San Jose, a church that is well over a hundred years old, the church committee, with the prompting of Patrick Smiley, decided they wanted to put a labyrinth on the floor. Unfortunately they didn't have enough room for a Chartres labyrinth, so Patrick agonized over making a Labyrinth that would fit, until it finally came together at the last minute. It's beautiful, it's fluid and it really compliments the round sanctuary with it's beautifully domed ceiling and balcony above. If you are ever in San Jose, you should stop by and visit it. The church is open during the week between 11am and 1 PM for daily labyrinth meditation. Call the church or check their website for exact times and events.

7 circuit labyrinth at the First Unitarian Church of San Jose, San Jose, CA. Designed for the church by Patrick Smiley and Steven Stein

Personally, I think switchbacks are a dynamic element that should be included whenever possible, especially if the labyrinth is going to be used for rituals and ceremonies.

In my experience, the switchbacks add more energy to the already working energies. Almost like a catalyst. I personally notice a big difference between a labyrinth with or without switchbacks. Especially when the labyrinth is Geo-oriented. Meaning oriented according to the Earth's directions. The opening of classic traditionally were oriented to the sun at the solstices with the opening facing east. I just hope that those who are building modern labyrinths are being so painstaking in the orientation. I can't stress this enough. It's a very important part of the process of creating a sacred space.

The orientation of the labyrinth should not be taken lightly. Building and working with labyrinths is something to be taken seriously. Creating a sacred space in your life is something to be protected. It is important to understand that once the initial building of a sacred space is complete. That space takes on a life of its own. If built and approached with respect, love and gratitude.

I find that when I work with switchbacks in a labyrinth, especially this series, moving back and forth between the directions, east, south, west and north, It feels like the energy is blending as it grows. The energies blend and there is a sort of gathering feel to how the paths run. Especially when you make that last turn, as you go around the outside curve, toward the goal and find yourself on the long sweep round the wheel ending a the goal. Even though you are moving widdershins, there is a gathering of the energy that you have been blending as you walk the outer paths. At least this is my experience.

My long time study of labyrinths has always made the Chartres one of the most fascinating to me. The switchbacks add a texture to the labyrinth that creates a much deeper meditative walk. Almost like giving your conscious mind something to do while you tap into your subconscious mind. Therefore I felt led to put switchbacks in my discovered patterns as well. The result was more than I could have planned on my own. The more I study labyrinths in general the more fascinated I am by these ancient magical spaces. It seems I now have a whole new set of patterns to study.

AI-6: Aquarian Labyrinth - 6 circuits

AL-6S: Aquarian Labyrinth - 6 circuits with switchbacks

Above is the 6 circuit Aquarian Labyrinth both with and without switchbacks done in a circle design to illustrate how the switchbacks give it a completely different character and feel. Interesting how the patterns esthetics change when it is made into a circle and opposed to organically.

Although I love the subject of switchbacks, I am not going to go into a lot of detail here. I will add more pattern pictures later on both with and without switchbacks.

As the patterns get bigger they also get more complicated. You will see what I mean when you see them and especially if you decide to make them. There is a method to the madness however. Study the patterns provided when laying out a circular labyrinth and it will make more sense once you do it. This is something that can be worked out on your own. Kind of your own discovery.

Chartres labyrinth pattern. For an in depth study of the Chartres Labyrinth, I suggest "Walking a Sacred Path" – Lauren Artress

Expanding Seed Patterns

Expanding the size of a labyrinth is not as hard as it might seem from the surface. Since a labyrinth is considered sacred geometry, it is very simple to expand or contract, a labyrinth pattern.

Let's go back to the seed patterns we looked at before.

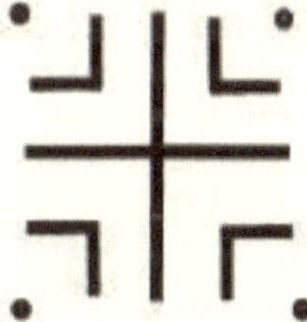

Classic Seed Pattern - will create the cretan labyrinth

The above seed pattern is the most commonly used. This pattern will make one of the oldest and most common patterns in the world, the Cretan 7 circuit labyrinth.

When the corners or L's are increased in number and then invoked to create a labyrinth, the number of circuits will increase by 4. So if you were to add a corner where each dot is now and then move the dots out an equal space from the corners, and drew it from there, you would have an 11 circuit labyrinth. If you were to add switchbacks to this pattern, you would have the Chartres labyrinth.

The Aquarian Labyrinth is no different. If you expand the seed pattern shown below as described above, you would get a 10 circuit continuous path labyrinth.

It felt a little spooky when I first expanded the original pattern of 6 circuits and it still worked out, as in all the paths worked. It just flowed like the first one did. Very naturally, very organically. The first expansion made it 10. Then I expanded it again bringing it to 14, it wasn't until a year later that I expanded it to 18.

When I expanded it to 18 it was very interesting to see that the opening to the goal became 10 and the goal to the exit became 8. 18 is a magical number. For 1 plus 8 is 9, and 9 plus 9 is 18...

It is important that I mention here, when I count circuits I am not counting the goal, just as you don't count the goal as a circuit in a traditional labyrinth.

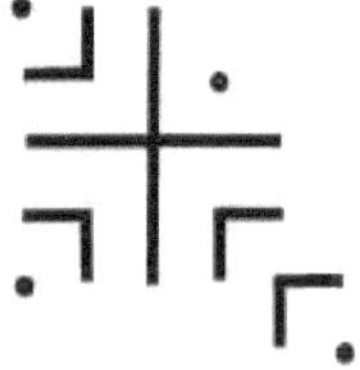

6 circuit Aquarian Labyrinth seed pattern

I have already shown you how to draw both a classic Cretan which is a 7 circuit and a 6 circuit Aquarian, so now all you need to understand is how to expand them.

From a 6 circuit, the next multiplication is 10, then 14, and then 18. All you have to do is add to your seed pattern then play connect the dots. Shown below is a sample of how the next multiplication looks, without switchbacks. Again, draw the seed pattern and play connect the dots according to the instructions earlier in this book. I suggest you draw each one. And "walk" them with your finger to see what I'm talking bout with the energies. Pay attention to how you feel with each one.

AL-10: Aquarian Labyrinth - 10 Circuits

AL-10S: Aquarian Labyrinth - 10 Circuits with Switchbacks

As you become more familiar with these patterns they will become like old friends, with different personalities all their own. Although they all come from a similar start, they all have something different to teach. And they all have something different to say. Walk and listen.

AL-14: Aquarian Labyrinth - 14 Circuits

AL-14S: Aquarian Labyrinth - 14 Circuits with switchbacks

AL-18: Aquarian Labyrinth - 18 Circuit

AL-18S: Aquarian Labyrinth - 18 Circuit with switchbacks

Chapter 5 – Walking the Labyrinth

If you have never walked a labyrinth before you may feel intimidated at first look. I too was a little apprehensive the first time I stood at the mouth of the meandering pathway.

The first thing to know is that you can not get lost, there is only one path, and no choices once the journey has begun. You just simply follow the path and you will wind up at the goal or center. No real thought it required the path is laid before you. There is no wrong way to walk the labyrinth. Some people walk very quickly passing others on the way as if on a mission, some walk slow and methodically. Children tend to want to run it.

Some people like to ask the labyrinth a question like an oracle, and some may have a problem they would like to solve. However you feel you would like to engage the labyrinth is up to you. Like I said there is no wrong way to walk the labyrinth.

Please be mindful

when approaching a labyrinth. Keep in mind, this is a sacred space. Watch your words, watch your thoughts. I believe labyrinths in general amplify your intentions. Just keep that in mind.

Stand at the opening, close your eyes, take a deep breath. Open your eyes and take the first step, no two journeys will be the same.

Shade dappled Labyrinth Pathways at Wilbur Hot Springs - Williams CA

Being in the moment

One of the biggest aspects I have learned about walking the labyrinth is that being in the moment is how we connect with it, ourselves and the natural world. And being in the moment is how we discover the secrets of the labyrinth, ourselves and the universe.

When we are in the moment, we are able to hear the wee small voice inside. The one that is your true compass. The one that is your higher self, your true self. The one you came here to be. Since it is so important to be in the moment, I noticed something about the differences of the classic patterns and the Aquarian pattern. The classic pattern has one path that goes all the way to the goal, which is where answers to questions are received and where change takes place, then one goes back over the same path they took to get there. Metaphorically, this seems counterproductive. Many of the great teachers teach being in the present, and once you have let go of something, not to rehash it, or go over it again. To be free from a painful situation of the past one has to be in the present moment. Not at the whim of the emotions that are attached to the trauma that has caused the pain and is being cleared. Once one has experienced and learned from an experience, they shouldn't have to go over it again, unless they truly have not released

everything, in which case they can start the process
again.

The first time I walked the Aquarian labyrinth path, I
noticed how the energy seemed clean, for lack of a
better word, upon leaving the goal. This brought me
to spending some time with that energy and testing
it with classic labyrinths. My personal perception
was that the energy flowed in a river like effect. It
felt to me, as if the goal/heart served as a pool or
vessel where energy could mingle and linger.
However that was as far as it could go. Since a
river or stream can only flow in one direction, and
energy flows, very much the same way as water. I
felt intuitively that the energy felt stagnant, in the
center of a traditional labyrinth, because it has
nowhere to go. Like water, energy must flow or it
gets blocked and causes a dam where it backs up.
Releasing the energy flow is like pulling the plug on
a bathtub drain.

With a continuous path labyrinth, the energy may
linger and spin for a while at the heart, but it
eventually continues and flow out of the labyrinth
where it can choose to go back in and recycle or
out into the universe to be used in the manner of
the intent given by those who created the energy
flow. This constant flow is what causes the 'clean
feeling that I mentioned earlier. The only way
energy can flow in such a way is by allowing the
flow to take place, which brings us full circle back to

being in the moment. If we are stuck in the past or fearful of the future we are not allowing the flow that is happening now. It is only by being fully in the now that the flow can cleanse the trauma and pain of the past to bring you into an empowered future.

Energy Flow – Chi, Prana, Universal Life Force, Awen

While going to massage school, I learned about what Traditional Chinese Medicine refers to as Chi. Chi is the life force, the breath, the Prana.

In TCM (Traditional Chinese Medicine) Chi is what runs through the meridians of our bodies. When imbalances in the meridians occur, disease can take place in the physical body.

The Earth herself has a similar meridians commonly known as ley-lines. These ley-lines move energy around the earth and keep her electromagnetic field working and in balance. The earth too can get energy build ups or blocks. I have known a few people in my travels who worked with these earth energies to alleviate the blockages wherever possible. I do believe working with the combination of earth energies and the labyrinth is not only healing to us, but also healing to the earth.

Many ancient labyrinths and earthen mounds have been confirmed to be on intersections of such lines.

The energy that flows through a labyrinth, weather it be classical or contemporary, is the same type of energy. Depending upon what your personal beliefs are will depend on what you call this flow of energy. The flow of Universal Life Force Energy, or whatever you want to call it, could be a lifelong study all on it's own.

I have heard Reiki masters call it Universal Life Force Energy. Although I too am a Reiki Master/Teacher I personally work with Awen, which is an ancient Celtic/Gaelic word meaning inspirational flow. Very often associated with Bards and writing poetry or music. It is this same flow of creativity that flows within us all. The same flow and spark of inspiration that began our life in this incarnation. It has been known for all ages by all people and we are now realizing in our modern world, what our ancestors have known for ages.

You may be asking why I am going into so much depth here about energy and energy flow. Because it is important to understand working with subtle energies to facilitate and become familiar with the work associated with the labyrinth. The more you work with labyrinths the more you will experience this flow of energy and how those energies differ from labyrinth to labyrinth. Not only in the style or size but also the location. The labyrinth does not have to be directly on a vortex, but if it is, the energies are much more intense.

One way flow – "Continuous Path"

One of my favorite aspects of these patterns is, no backtracking. As I think I stated earlier, personally I think it's counter productive to use the same path twice. I know I tend to repeat myself but I do believe this is important. As nice as it is to give our fellow brothers and sisters the room to pass, either going in or coming out, as you must do with a traditional labyrinth, it tends to change the flow. I'm sure I could write a lot more on this subject alone, but my reason for mentioning it here is to make you aware of it so you can notice how you feel when you walk a traditional pattern as opposed to walking the Aquarian pattern. I find that passing people on the path tends to break my concentration and therefore my energy tends to get scattered rather than staying focused. I have looked at this from a metaphorical view as well. Earlier I talked about the flow of the Labyrinth akin to the flow of a river. I know from my experience that when I try to swim upstream I get worn out, however, if I relax in the water and allow the flow of the river to take me there, I am less likely to get worn out and arrive on the shore safely. Of course we still have to watch out for those big rocks but that could be another writing all together, just remember this is a metaphor after all. We find this to be the same in life, if we allow the flow of our life, our personal sacred Awen to flow in the river of our lives and we move with, instead of fighting against the current, we arrive right where we want to or need to be at the right time. When we move with the current, we don't wear ourselves out and we can use that energy in more productive ways. What are you resisting? Whatever we resist persists. So if we are having trouble getting in the flow, maybe we need to look at what it is we are resisting and ask ourselves why. If we can find the root cause of the resistance, and change our way of thinking about it to where we are no longer resisting and start focusing on what we want and not what we don't want, then the current will flow in our lives and the stagnation will clear itself out, ending up with us being more productive with less effort.

I have spent much time with Labyrinths in general, but I have also spent a lot more time with the Aquarian Labyrinth and I have allowed it to teach me as I go along. One of the lessons of this Labyrinth is yet another metaphor. When you stand at the opening of the Aquarian Labyrinth, you will see two paths before you. Many people choose or feel led to take the path on the left. I find many children tend to want to start on the right.

Since there are two paths right next to each other, it is very easy to start over right away by just doing one more u-turn. Many times in walking this path, when I get to the end, coming out of the path on the right, I turn around and go right back in. Sometimes I will do this several times in a row. This is also useful when dancing the labyrinth. The first person in the chain will dance out of the opening and turn around and go right back in again, those who wish to sit out the next round don't have to go back in. I love it when we have enough people to fill the labyrinth and have overflow of people in a long chain working together to bring peace and healing to the world by their sacrifice of dance. Oh yes, I was talking about metaphors wasn't I? Well this flow is yet one more of those, this flow is that of recycling, or reincarnation. The flow out of one life and and back in to a new one. Didn't quite get it at the end of life? Need to go back and try again? No problem!! Just rinse and repeat. I love this concept! Just one more thing to consider while dancing the path of the Aquarian pattern. This also emulates the reincarnation of water. As the clouds come and and create rain, then that rain flows down to the lower land where it gives life to everything in its path only to evaporate back up to the clouds to be reused and bless the earth again and again. As new lessons come to me it becomes easier and easier to understand how profound this pattern really is.

Energy Flow and the Sacred Circle

This next section will be familiar to people who follow a nature based spirituality. If you are one of those, you will probably already understand what I am going to talk about next.

If you are not familiar with working with subtle energies, this next section may seem a little foreign to you. I ask that you read this section with an open mind and to make a space of allowing within your heart. These are the same energies I work with as a bodyworker and Reiki Master/Teacher on a regular basis.

Basic energy exercise

The purpose of this exercise is to help you tune into the energies of the labyrinth as well as the various elements and directions. These energies are mostly elemental energies of, Air – Fire – Water – Earth collectively. Basically we are creating a sacred circle every time we walk the labyrinth. Whether we are consciously aware of it or not.

The following exercise will help you to recognize these energies more intimately.

In working with labyrinths particularly the Aquarian patterns, I noticed an interesting energy flow. I spoke before about setting up a labyrinth to be Geo-oriented. This usually means that the opening faces East. I will attempt to describe this energy gathering by using this geographical orientation as my basis.

The following is written using the 6 circuit Aquarian labyrinth pattern with switchbacks. As pictured below. If you don't have access to this labyrinth pattern for walking, you can use the picture below and walk it with your finger. You may be surprised at how effective just using a finger labyrinth can be. You may wish to do this exercise outside and situate yourself so that you are sitting facing west. This way you can imagine that you are sitting in the center of the labyrinth when you get there on paper and meditate a while.

For this exercise we will be entering the labyrinth path on the left, take a moment to bring your awareness to how you feel. Physically, Mentally, Emotionally. Don't try to change it, just observe it. Also observe how the energy around you feels. You may wish to do a protection ritual however you choose. Call in your guides or any angels, saints or deities that you may work with regularly.

For the purpose of this energy exercise just observe the energy without trying to obtain an answer or change the flow. The purpose is just to observe and be sensitive to the various energies.

As you step onto the labyrinth path from the east tune into and notice the soft air energy. Observe how it makes you feel. You do not have to think about it or change it, just observe. Moving forward, the path makes an immediate left moving southward which is fire energy. As you move south, observe that energy as well. Notice how it feels in comparison to the east/air energy. Does it feel warmer, dryer, brighter? Now you come to the first switchback, which make another left and heads back toward the east/air again. As you are walking in this space between directions/elements, see if you can feel the two energies mingling together in this space and observe how the energy of the elements interact with each other. Remember air feeds fire so you may start to feel a bit warmer. When the path reaches the east, it will make a right and start heading toward the west/water, but not before it passes through the south/fire quadrant for the last time.

As you pass through the south, it is good to pause for a moment at the end of the south switchback and reflect on how the south/fire feels before moving in the west/water quadrant . You are now moving toward the west, the cooling of the water element here will make for an interesting dynamic which can sometimes be a little intense. Think of how water and fire interact. What do they make? Usually steam. However too much water is capable of putting out or quenching the fire. So as you weave back and forth between the two elements of fire and water in the next two switchbacks keep this in mind and see if the two balance themselves.

The path will continue in this way as it eventually comes around to north/earth and back to east/air again. Once again you will be observing the respective energies of north/earth and west/water as you work the switchbacks in those quadrants. As you leave those quadrants it's good to pause now and then to observe the feeling of that particular energy.

Finishing up in the East you will now begin the last long sweep that will slingshot you directly to the goal. As you walk this pattern widdershins, visualize bringing all of the elements together as if you are gathering the energies as you move toward the heart. Observe how they feel as you gather each one.

As you meandered around the outside circle in a deosil fashion you were invoking those elements/direction as you went, so now a cycle has completed within you. You are the catalyst for bringing these together as one. You are now the fifth element, Spirit. Notice that as you work the outside circle, you were moving in a deosil (clockwise) circle, this is the same direction that a sacred circle is drawn.

Once you are at the heart, once again observe what you are feeling, what you are experiencing, and how the energies feel.

Now sit at the center heart and take this opportunity to raise the energy you just gathered higher through deep breathing. As you breath feel the energy build and build until you feel you need to release it.

Release it by taking one last deep breath and on your exhale, imagine it releasing out all of your best intentions for the universe or a situation you are dealing with. As you let it go, just know that it will come to pass in a way which is in your best interest and the best interest of those involved. Be happy for those who will receive from your beautiful visualization.

What it really comes down to is intention, intention, intention. Whatever we put our attention to we draw to us, be it positive or negative, so be careful what you think about and occupy your mind with, and also watch what you say. Words are energy primed to become reality.

After you have spent as much time as you wish in the goal/center, you may now continue on the path to the exit. As you first walk widdershins and then deosil on the way out, consider giving thanks to the universe as you walk in those directions and give appreciation to the keepers of the directions/elements for the help/energy they have lent to your cause. This is also a good time to show appreciation or gratitude to you personal guide for protecting you during your spiritual work.

As you exit, acknowledge the labyrinth for the hidden gifts it reveals. Bring your awareness to how you feel, physically, mentally, emotionally. Stand at the opening/exit and observe how you feel in comparison to how you felt before you walked the labyrinth. Do you notice a difference? If so, what?

I hope you enjoyed this simple visualization. If you have one you would like to share, contact me, I would love to hear about it.

Note: The purpose of this text is not to tell you how to or who to pray to. It is simply a guideline of how I have found to work with the Aquarian Labyrinth patterns in general and the energies I find there.

If you don't understand deosil and widdershins, I will explain it in a simple form here.

The direction of deosil is clockwise or sun-wise, it is considered to be the positive, building, planting side of the coin when it comes to creating a sacred circle. A sacred circle is drawn in the deosil direction, at least in the Northern hemisphere.

The direction of widdershins is counter-clockwise or anti-sun-wise. It is considered to be the negative, tear-down, reaping side of the coin when it comes to creating a sacred circle. A sacred circle is diminished or un-drawn in the widdershins direction, at least in the northern hemisphere. I hope that helps.

Walking with intention

As with any magickal or psychic workings intention is everything. In reality we don't need a labyrinth or any other magickal tools to create or manifest something into our life. Thought is enough. Herbs, stones, candles, colors etc are all wonderful tools for helping you to focus, but when you are able to manifest with just thought alone or work a spell with thought alone, you will understand what I mean by thought is enough. Focus of pure intention can manifest very quickly with practice. One way to practice is by walking the labyrinth.

Note: *When I say throughout this text, "Walking the labyrinth." Even though I have written the following exercises as if you had a full sized Aquarian Labyrinth in your yard, Please know that I also consider running the labyrinth with your finger, either on paper or a labyrinth board, the same as walking it. The energy builds regardless of the size of the tool, again it comes back to intention. This can also help with your visualization skills. If you visualize walking a real labyrinth while you run a finger labyrinth, your inner vision will get stronger.*

If you have gotten this far in the text I'm sure it is clear that I follow an earth based belief system. I will not categorize it, as it cannot be categorized. My beliefs are my own and I do not try to sell anyone on it, nor do I wish to tell anyone else how to believe, worship or pray. I am a solitary practitioner so sometimes Its hard for me to share in a group setting since beliefs are so varied, and it is not my intention to offend anyone. Whatever your belief system is, feel free to change any of my suggestion to suit your purpose. If you too are of an earth based belief, just know this is how I do it and feel free to change it to suit your ways. Having said that, I will now share with you a few simple ideas that have worked for me over the years. Some of them I learned along the way and some of them were taught to me by the Aquarian Labyrinth patterns.

Intention

I know that I have already touched on this subject, but I would like to go into more detail here.

When we walk a labyrinth with intention something quite majickal happens. It is almost as if the labyrinth feels or knows your intention and magnifies it. Not only does it magnify it out into the world, but it also magnifies it in your life. Teachers have used the pebble in the pond for a model of cause and effect. Upon looking at a labyrinth, it is easy to see how it looks like someone dropped a pebble in a pond. I can't help but think, that this is a model for how our thought energy travels out into the world. Since many of the metaphorical lessons of the labyrinth work in emulation of real life. I many times meditate on this image of the labyrinth being alike to a pond and the ripples of our conscious thought are the ripples on that pond. Those ripples go out into the world and have the ability to change what cannot be seen, resulting in change that can be seen. In my opinion, the model of the pebble in the pond is the best description of how majick works.

I am not going to go into detail here on how or why majick works and I am not going to give a quantum physics lesson either. If you have not studied on these subjects I encourage you to do so in the future. It is most enlightening as to how the universe works and how everything is energy. If you are not at a level where this makes sense to you, may I suggest you go back and read some books on, at the very least, basic quantum physics.

Once you get your head around it, you may look at things very differently.

When setting an intention it is very important to be crystal clear as to what you are requesting the outcome to be. Energy doesn't have a conscious or a thought pattern as we operate. Energy is what it is programed to be. Therefore, it is important to make your program positive and loving. It is also important to think through what that outcome might mean for others around you or connected with the situation. Will transposing my will in this situation over the will of others cause adverse effects? Basically, will it have a negative effect on anyone? If so, are you willing and or able to take responsibility for your part? These are things I remind people of when they wish to act impulsively, or wish to force their will over the will of someone else. I'm just saying you must be careful of what you put out there, for Karmic law is always in effect. If you have thought it through and you are now clear on what it is you are drawing into your life, and its possible outcome then it is time to move forward with your walk.

Before your walk, sit in a comfortable position. Close your eyes as if to get into a meditative state. Now think about your intention, and what you wish to draw to yourself. In your minds eye, see exactly what your goal is. Get a vivid picture of it. See it, feel it, taste it, smell it, touch it!! The idea here is to get as vivid a picture of your desire as possible.

Once you have your vivid picture, stand at the opening of the labyrinth and ask for guidance as to how to accomplish this goal. Clear your mind and step onto the path. As you walk think about the goal, but keep your senses open to receive an answer. Depending on how you receive information, will depend on how you will receive this information. Some will see images, some will hear, or smell things, pay attention or you just might miss it.

By the time you reach the heart you will have consciously or unconsciously gathered energy, like the example earlier in this writing, regarding your goal. It is now time to let it go.

Upon reaching the heart it is important to be ready to let it go. Feel all the energy you have gathered and allow it to swirl throughout your body and being. Now in whatever way feels natural to you, visualize this energy rippling out into the world. Going back to the pebble in the pond, I find it helpful to use that model to visualize my intention moving out into the world and beyond.

As I mentioned before, if you open your eyes and look out over the labyrinth, you will notice how it reminds you of ripples on a pond. I don't believe this is a coincidence. I believe it is how this energy that we work with in the labyrinth travels out into the world to create whatever it is that we wish to create. We are creative beings after all. Allow the energy to flow through you as it leaves, without taking your personal energy with it, we don't want you drained at the end of the exercise.

Some of the ways I release energy is yawning. For me it is a physiological side effect of working with energy. Most of the time when doing a Reiki session I begin to yawn, especially when the client starts to release emotionally. As I yawn I visualize the energy leaving through my breath. Another way to release excess energy is to raise your hands over your head, planting your feet firmly on the ground and visualizing the energy leaving through your hands and feet. Sometimes this can have a lighting-bolt effect where you may feel very energized afterward.

Yet another way to release excess energy is to simply place your hand on the earth and projecting it down to the ground. Also known as grounding. If the energy is really strong, lay down on the ground so you have full contact with the earth. You can release that extra energy any way you feel most comfortable. Send it out with love and it will be sure to come good and meander back to you, but with a magnified effect of love and healing.

Once you have released your intention, it is now time to accept the outcome as granted. As you walk the last short bit of the labyrinth path, find your place of gratitude. Use the exit path as a path of thanksgiving. Gratitude is the glue that binds it all together.

You can thank the universe, your angels or guides, or whoever – whatever you feel comfortable working with in regards to a higher power.

Once you find yourself at the mouth of the labyrinth once again, it is good to take a moment to think about and acknowledge the work that has been done before continuing on with your day.

Did you receive any messages, or images as you walked? If you journal, now would be a good time to sit and journal about your experience. This is a great way of looking back at the moment you started to manifest this particular thing and you can see how long it takes to come to pass.

Even if you feel you didn't sense anything profound, know within yourself that changes are being made on your behalf. If you are new to this type of work you may be on the fence as to if it will even make a difference. Trust in your own power to change the universe and you will be surprised what you can accomplish.

Please feel free to come up with your own way of walking with intention. The key is being clear on your goal.

If your self talk starts with doubt at anytime before it manifests itself, just remind your subconscious that you walked the labyrinth about it and it has already come to pass in the energetic reality, even if you can't tangibly see it, YET. Then place it back into the care of the universe once again.

Sometimes the work is so simple that we have to remind ourselves that we even, "did the work..."

If these exercises come easy to you, be thankful within your being. For thanksgiving is the key that unlocks the power of the universe. This is a good thing!

Walking with the Spirit

Do you connect daily with the spirit? Maybe I should mention here what I mean when I say spirit. Most of us who have a belief system of some-kind, usually have an angel or guide that we follow, or work with as life presents itself. Someone from the spirit world who aids us and guides us.

If you are the one who does not work with or does not wish to work with a spirit guide or the like, you may wish to skip over this section.

The following are suggestions of what can be accomplished when working with our guide(s). For the simplicity of clarification I will furthermore refer to any spiritual entity such as angels, guides, ascended masters etc, to simply "Spirit". Who you work with is up to you.

This is similar to waking with intention, however, when we are walking with the spirit, we are allowing spirit to guide not only our steps but as time progresses, our intentions. As we work the labyrinth with the help and guidance of spirit, many times our very intention will change. For instance, after working with spirit and the labyrinth for a time, we may come to a place of seeing the bigger picture. We may see clearly how our ripple in the pond affects those around us and beyond. Once these realizations are made, it is then up to us to change our course to match that new realization an in turn, new intention.

I don't intend to make this complicated. And you may already understand how to do this. If not, hold tight and lets see if we can learn something.

In order to work with spirit, it is helpful to already have a relationship with the particular energy/entity you are going to work with. If you do not have such relationship, I suggest you move forward with the following exercise once you have established such relationships. Moving forward I am going to presume you have an established, previously mentioned, relationship.

Sit just outside the labyrinth, and connect with spirit. Once you have made contact in whatever way you usually do, now is a good time to ask any of a million questions. I could go into great detail here and go step by step to overload you with details, however I don't wish to take away your joy of discovery. Take this simple following example and fine tune it to make it your own. The idea is to connect with spirit and basically ask a question. If you don't know what to ask, may I suggest, "What do I need to know at this time?". Sometimes we don't know what we need and instead of just powering through such times, it is best to ask spirit for some guidance. Once you have a good idea of what to ask, move to the mouth of the labyrinth and ask your question, then start to walk.

Walk fast or slow, it's up to you. You may even find yourself stopping along the way. Relax and tune into spirit. Be sensitive, especially in the beginning. Just keep working with it and it will get easier.

Some of the ways you may receive messages from spirit, inner vision, inner voice, inner feeling, inner knowing. There are names for the four psychic senses, they are, Clair-voyance, Clair-audience, Clair-sentience and Clair-cognizance. Everyone is born with these abilities to some extent, however these abilities can be developed the more you use them. I realize that some may think they don't have any abilities in these areas. This is not true. They are just not developed it yet. Work with it, it will come to you. As you tune into spirit regularly it will get easier and easier, until it becomes second nature.

Rest at the heart to see if you receive anything special. Sometimes it will be like a lighting-bolt, and other times it may not come to you until hours or even days later. Be patient – Allow. Just as you did in the intention exercise, be grateful for what you received during this walk even if the outcome is not real clear just yet. Gratitude makes the difference!

Keep in mind that sometimes the hardest thing to do is listen to the wee small voice which is the polite voice of spirit. We live in a world that is always coming at us with information and "stuff". After a while it becomes white noise and it can be easy to lose contact with the input that can be of great importance to us. Pure, free input of spirit which we have available to us without electronics. Try to focus in on that wee small voice deep inside, even if that voice is a wee small feeling inside. Spirit is polite and nudges ever so gently in the direction you wish to go. After you work with these abilities a while, it will become easier. Just know that learning to listen is the most important skill to learn if you are planning to work with spiritual energies.

Walking in Prayer

One of the most effective ways I have found to walk the labyrinth is by walking in prayer. This can be as simple as having a song on your lips or as elaborate as reading or reciting a detailed prayer. During these prayer walks I find myself stopping at undetermined spots on the labyrinth. Sometimes to contemplate, sometimes to connect closer with spirit, sometimes just to listen.

At times an affirmation will come to me for a specific situation in life. Walking the labyrinth while saying affirmations has been beneficial in creating the energy that I am working to accomplish. Whether that be healing, manifesting something physical, like money or improving my outlook on a situation. I find walking the labyrinth while using affirmations has been very successful for me, I encourage you to try it.

Some of my favorite affirmations come from Louise Hay. You can heal your life, has changed my life literally. Her work has been insurmountable in the moving forward of our collective consciousness. If you are new to working with affirmations, may I suggest you start with her work.

In using affirmations, once you have come to a point of knowing what you are requesting, then you can be clear in asking. You can ask as you walk the labyrinth, or you can wait until you get the goal and ask there. It is entirely up to you, it's your walk! The only strong suggestion I make, it that you express your thankfulness for receiving the request as you walk the exit path.

In my opinion, prayer is no more than making requests of the universe for things you wish to change in your present situation. I don't believe prayer is begging some unseen god to throw you a morsel from his table. I believe prayer to be the human soul petitioning the universe for what is needed. The answer to prayer is not based on whether you are good or bad. It is based on belief, or faith, and the law of attraction.

For one to have belief or faith that something is going to change in their favor, we first have to petition for what is is we need or desire. Then it is a matter of phrasing it in such a way that you are showing faith or belief that you will receive what you are requesting. By making your request in the positive you open the door for positive to find you. Like attracts like. Your words are the first physical manifestation of thought. That is why the spoken word has power. Words are sound and sound is a physical vibration. It takes a physical vibration to affect the physical world. When we speak our prayers, we are not only affecting the physical world by creating the vibration of our desire in the world with our voice, but we are also affecting and basically changing our bodies to align with our prayer.

If I have lost you with this portion, I apologize, I just assume you know what I'm talking about. Like I stated earlier, you may need to go and do some studying on your own to understand some of these things, depending on what you have studied prior to reading this.

As we walk the labyrinth prayerfully it is important to tune into spirit as we walk in order to make that connection that we seek. I suppose it would even be possible to pray the rosary as you walk if you so choose. In a way the labyrinth becomes a sort of rosary. In that we use it as a catalyst to better connect with spirit. The more you connect, the stronger that connection becomes. The idea is that if you need a tool to connect better with spirit until your connection is strong enough to connect without a tool, then by all means use the tool that best suits you and your particular practice.

In my personal practice I have found that "I AM" statements have been the most effective.

For instance, if I am praying for lets say; healing. I might phrase my statement something like this.

"I am thankful that the healing that I have requested has been given and received. I now accept this healing that my body may continue to be whole. I am Health, I am Strength, I am one with the universe and I am a complete and whole."

You see we always talk about the issue as if it were resolved. This insures that we are exercising our faith or belief, that what we have requested has come to pass. By accepting it now even before you see physical evidence, is how we align our vibration with the thing we are drawing to us. That way we become a match for the thing that we desire.

Of course there is a school of thought that subscribes to the idea that if you request healing, then you are in the very act of making the request, admitting that there is an issue or problem in the present and that it creates an opposite effect, like two magnets moving in opposite directions.

That is something my dear ones that you are going to have to come to realization about on your own.

The simplest affirmations are simply what I call, I am, statements.

One line affirmations confirm your desire within your subconscious that you are, or possess exactly what you are claiming to be or have. Such as, "I am the luckiest person I know.", or " I am healthy, wealthy and wise." That has been one of my personal favorites for several years, thank you Benjamin Franklin.

The most important part of the whole process is being thankful. Learning to be happy with what you have presently is always the best way to appreciate what is coming your way.

I would like to say that I do not wish to tell you how to pray. My intention is merely to give you some suggestions of what can be done if you need it. If you have a regular prayer life I hope that you can find a way to incorporate your way of praying into a practice with the labyrinth. You may be surprised as to what transpires.

It takes a lot of rocks to build a labyrinth!!

Chapter 6 – Path and the Spiral

All labyrinths are riddled with meanings and metaphors. As for this writing, I will speak specifically about the Aquarian Labyrinth patterns.

I was thinking about how this labyrinth has one continuous path and how our lives emulate Labyrinths in general. When we examine what has already been said about labyrinths and their symbolism there is much talk about the path being like our lives or the path of our life. How we are all on a path. We don't really know where we are going or how we will get there, but we are going. And with observation and trust in the system that is this universe we get there, wherever THERE is, welcome to the human mystery.

I was reflecting on what Melissa Gayle West said in her book – Exploring the Labyrinth – A Guide for Healing and Spiritual Growth. Pg 9 - "Walking the Labyrinth deepens one's spiritual path, whatever that path may be. The Labyrinth can be a path of prayer, taking us – no matter whom or what we worship – to the center: the center of creation and the center of your own hearts and souls. The labyrinth welcomes us all with open arms, inviting us to walk directly with spirit."

This is a great quote! Like all other labyrinths, the Aquarian Labyrinth not only takes you to the center of creation (Self, God, etc.) it can, if you allow it, change you as you reach the heart. I look at the heart as a place of change. Once you cross over the center threshold – you are different; better; you continue on your journey all the way out - once the "change" happens, there is no reason to pass back over the past, or to re-trod over old ground as humans often do within themselves. The heart could be looked upon as a place of enlightenment. The place where lightning strikes.

In this life we don't get the opportunity to go back over our past and change or rearrange them – except in our minds, and as we know this can cause us to have no peace with the past. We can either come from a place of learning and acceptance, of our life and past experiences - which would benefit us, even heal us. Or we can come from a place of resistance and blame, which can eventually become toxic to us. We can either learn from and accept our experiences or they can become bitter memories; the choice is ours.

The point of all of that is to say this; we don't get the chance to go back and change or fix it physically, so there is no need to walk the same path twice. Many times just letting go and allowing, gives room for a situation to work itself out. My

Grandmother used to tell me this when I was young and fretting about things of the world and how I wanted to "Change" them. The problem with that thinking is that whatever the issue is, it is already perfect. Our only job is looking at it and seeing what we can glean from it. What can we learn from a "bad" situation and how does that process change us? For, once we change we never look at things the same again.

The path is something that we are on, and there is no stopping it. There are those who have tried, but alas to their own demise. I would consider that choice the ultimate resistance. What does your path look like today? What can you glean from it today? Play the Pollyanna game if you have to. If we can find a way to glean something positive from each and every day, we will be well on our way to loving the life you have, which will have a profound impact on receiving the life you dream of.

This brings me to spirals. Spirals are a magical thing. I know there have been times when I started drawing them and filled an entire page. Spirals can be found in all ancient cultures. Carved into stone or earth, painted on cave walls and pottery. Spirals are sacred. When we enter the circle of a sacred or holy place such as a Tipi, sweat lodge, or medicine wheel, we are required to follow the circle around in a deosil direction, as a sign of respect for "The Old Ones" and the sacred circle or spiral of life. In doing so we honor all who are part of the great circle of life, the great spiral of the universe. We have all seen pictures from space and seen how even our Milky-way is in the form of a spiral. Spirals can even appear in every one of the four elements, Air, Fire, Water, Earth. So naturally they are considered sacred.

Spirals are a natural occurrence. There are water spirals known as whirlpools, and water in general flows in spirals. Air spirals known as whirlwinds or in full force, tornadoes. Space is a spiral, and the way planets are formed is also a spiral. The planets of our solar system travels around the sun in a spiral. Since the Sun is moving towards Lambda Hercules at 20 kilometers per second or 12 miles per second. Or in units "per hour": 72,000 kilometers per hour or 45,000 miles per hour.

Earth is moving around the sun. The sun is moving within the Galaxy. The sun is revolving around the galactic center. The galaxy is moving within the local group. The local group is moving toward the Virgo Supercluster. The Virgo supercluster is moving through the universe. The universe is expanding, and this is all happening in a spiral. The DNA for all living things is a spiral. Many fruits and flowers also grow in spiral patterns.

In watching spirals we can become fascinated with it's simple flow, yet it takes just the right conditions to create this effect. The water and or wind and atmospheric conditions have to be just right for these phenomena to take place. Interesting how something so seemingly simple and common can be so complex.

Ancient people painted spirals on cave walls and carved them into rocks long ago. Which shows that there is something very primal and deep rooted in humans that connects us to the spiral. Deep down we understand the spiral of life and how completely disconnected we are in this time we live. We cry out for a time long past when the people of the world danced the spiral dance. When we root ourselves to the earth, loved and protected her.

Labyrinths too are spirals. If you work with labyrinths already, I'm sure you understand this. If you are new to labyrinths and labyrinth work you may have not put the two together just yet. The more you work with them the better you will understand this.

The most interesting thing to me about spirals, especially those we can observe like whirlpools and whirlwinds is that they seem to move by an unseen force. Through science we understand how the liquids of water and air move and respond to various atmospheric changes that would cause such events. Although we may explain it away through science, as humans we still tend to see the magic as it happens right before us.

When we look at Eastern philosophy and the study of chakras we see that even within our own bodies we have swirling vortexes of energy happening all the time. Chakras too are ever spinning spirals. When a body worker checks a person's chakras for imbalances, they often check the spin with a pendulum. If the spin is too small or too slow in comparison to the others, it can indicate an imbalance in the electromagnetic field and as a result can affect the physical body by creating imbalances also known as disorders or disease.

These are just some examples of swirls and spirals that happen in nature. But there are many more and we could fill a whole volume talking about such things. My point in mentioning it here is this. I wish to make you aware of these various swirling energies , they are important in the work that goes along with these labyrinth patterns. The spiral will take you safely to your inner self, then back out again. Feel the flow and allow the current to move you. Within this, spiraling flow we create sacred space.

The Labyrinth too is a sacred spiral which is good for yet another metaphor of the spiral of life. The next time you walk a labyrinth, I encourage you to think about this aspect. Think about how each of us is on a path. As we are on that path we can see other people on their own path. From your vantage point, it seems that you are each walking a separate path. However, when you backup or get a higher vantage point, you can see that you are all on the same path, just in different place on the same path. In this way, the path represents the path of life that we each must walk. We each have a goal in mind, yet we must make twists and turn along the way. Since we each step onto the path at a different time, the path will be different for each of us, just as life is different for each of us. Yet in that differences, we find sameness. Some may get there slowly, some may speed towards an unseen goal, yet we are all still on the same path. Some may turn right as yet others are turning left, yet we are all on the same path. Sometimes as we head down our path we feel as though we are moving far from our goal, yet other times it feels so close you can touch it but somehow it is just not obtainable, yet.

Notice how the path meanders left and right, right and left, even though you seem to be moving away from the heart, somehow you are traveling closer and closer to the heart. Just as any spiral will do. Until suddenly, there you are, at the heart, goal achieved.

Once we reach the heart it is not a place of stopping and turning around, it is now a place of contemplation. At the heart of the labyrinth is the place where we connect with our own heart. When we listen for the ancient wisdom that is within each of us. Where we can listen for that wee small voice which is ever present to guide and inspire us. It is then a place of sharing from your heart with the world.

AS I think about how spirals affect us, I realize that spirals especially labyrinths, create a shift in our perspective about things. This shift could be looked at as expressing the expansion of our consciousness. When I talk to people after they have walked the labyrinth, I usually ask them how they feel.. The answer I get the most is, " I feel like something shifted." or " I feel more grounded."

I believe this has to do with how spirals work within our bodies. The Chakra system is a system of energy vortexes at various points in our body. Many of us are familiar with the seven major chakras. However less people are aware of other chakras in locations such as the palms of our hands and the soles of our feet just as an example. Many of these minor chakras coincide with meridian lines used in Chinese medicine.

It is my belief that the swirling, spiraling action of the labyrinth energy, balances our spirals as we walk the pathways. If you have never noticed spirals in life before, I'm positive you will now start noticing how many of them are around us in our daily lives. Welcome to the sacred spiral of life!

Just as with learning, it doesn't do us any good unless we share what we have learned. For when we give it away, is when we truly receive in order to come to an even deeper understanding. It then becomes a place of sharing from our heart. Which is one of the most important lessons of the Aquarian Labyrinth. Sharing our hearts with others, and what we have learned along the way, just as the labyrinth has shared it's heart with us. When we share what we have learned, the spiral continues to grow, and thus, the great spiral dance of life goes on. The spiral within us all.

Giving thanks within the heart is powerful, but when that thanksgiving is carried through on the existing path back out into the world. I believe it becomes a catalyst that clears a path of newer and deeper connection with the divine spiral in all life. I encourage you to keep this in mind as you walk. You may come away with a different perspective of how you view people, and yourself.

This can become an exercise for a group. To walk the labyrinth through the eyes of, "We are all on the same path". Then share with each other, some of the insights you may have had during your walk.

"Our sense of obligation and loyalty needs to be to the earth and our community." - John Trudell

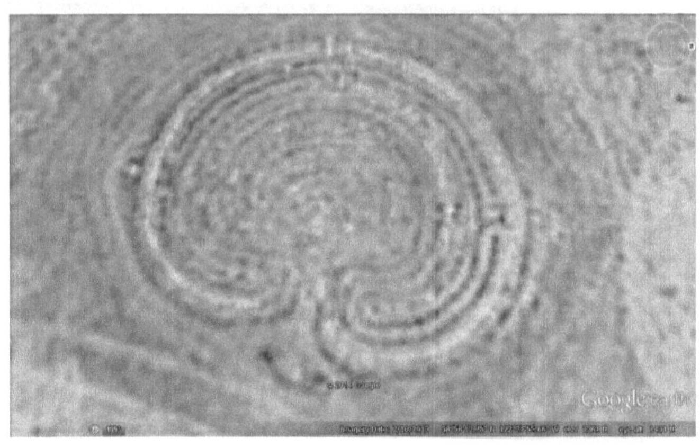

AL-14S - As seen from space according to
GoogleEarth.com. Please note this labyrinth no
longer exist.

Chapter 7 – The outer labyrinth – left path

AS I look out over the 14 circuit Aquarian pattern labyrinth in my backyard, I can't help but look at it and marvel at how it is two labyrinths in one. The path on the left is a longer path than the one on the right. The longer labyrinth goes from the entrance to the goal, the shorter leads from the goal to the exit. Depending upon which path you start out on will determine whether you are on the long or the short path, remember, this path can be walked either way. However, for simplicity sake. I will be referring to the path on the Left as being the Entrance and the path on the Right to be the Exit. Personally I am drawn to walk the long path first, but sometimes I walk it the other way. It really depends upon how the labyrinth communicates with me at that particular moment.

The left path – or – the Outer Labyrinth

For the following example, we will be using the 14 circuit Aquarian Labyrinth.

As we approach the mouth of the labyrinth, notice there are two paths side by side. Although both paths lead to the heart, the path on the left is a longer path. This path is longer for a few reasons.

The first reason for the extra length is because it is two circuits larger than the inner labyrinth.

Another reason it's longer is because of the switchbacks at the four points of the circle. These switchbacks are reminiscent of the Chartres labyrinth. This longer path creates an eight circuit labyrinth that meanders first in a counter clockwise direction, and then switches on itself to meander in a clockwise direction which sets the Walker up to make a final counter clockwise sweep to the heart.

These eight circuits deposits us at the heart, which completes the first portion of our walking experience.

The outer labyrinth is slightly reminiscent of the Chartres labyrinth in Chartres cathedral in France. However, on closer examination, it is easy to see that the two are so different that they are almost opposite one another.

I do not wish to give an exact comparison to how they are alike and/or different. Instead I will just point out some of the more obvious ways they are different.

The first difference is that the outer labyrinth on the Aquarian pattern has eight circuits, which could be expanded to ten if the entire labyrinth was made to be eighteen circuits, and the Chartres has eleven. This brings up the point of the odd number of circuits in a traditional labyrinth and the even number of circuits of the Aquarian patterns. No matter how big or small the pattern is expanded or contracted, this remains the same and is the main reason for the further differences in the two patterns. This stems from the difference in the the seed pattern and how it sets up the layouts of the various patterns. When either pattern is expanded or contracted they will all expand or contract by denominations of four. Classic patterns will expand by 7, 11, 15, 19 and so on. The Aquarian patterns will expand by 6, 10, 14, 18 and so on. Although a labyrinth any larger than eighteen would not only take up an enormous amount of space, as in acreage, it would also take a lot of care to maintain it.

When studying the switchbacks of the Chartres, it is interesting to notice how the number of switchback delineates are not an even number at the corners. Notice that the top and bottom points are made up of four switchbacks and the right and left pins are made up of three switchbacks. Upon examination it's easy to figure out that this was done to make it come out "even". The other thing I find interesting about the layout of the switchbacks is how the left one skips one circuit from the outside ring and the one on the right skips two circuits from the outside ring. Again this seems to be an attempt to "Balance" the wheel.

When studying the Aquarian Labyrinth, it is interesting that there are even numbers of circuits, even number of switchbacks and the number of circuits skipped on the left and right corners is the same. Maybe this is why this pattern feels balanced.

Chapter 8 – The Heart

In this chapter we will focus on the heart of the
Aquarian Labyrinth. In traditional labyrinths, the
center of the pattern is called the goal. For the
purposes of the Aquarian Labyrinth, calling it a goal
just didn't feel right. Therefore we call it the Heart.
And since the outer labyrinth is a path of love, it just
seemed to make sense.

The center of almost every labyrinth that I studied,
only had one pathway connecting to it. The center
of the Aquarian labyrinth has two pathways
attached to it. One leading into the goal and one
leading out. This seemed reminiscent of how a
human heart is, blood goes in, blood goes out and
it is a continuous loop system. Sound familiar?

Whichever path we came in on, weather it be the
long path or the short, we can then leave the center
taking the other path or we can turn around and
take the same path that we just came in on, just as
one would in a classic labyrinth.

Spring in the AL-14S/ The animals keep it well tended, if you don't mind moving the rocks back every few days.

Chapter 9 – The inner labyrinth – right path

This chapter will focus on the path on the right, or the inner labyrinth. For this example we will be using the Aquarian 14 circuit pattern. Below are two examples of walking the path on the right. The first example starts at the heart and moves outward and the second example starts at the mouth and works its way to the Heart.

The right path – or – the inner labyrinth

Starting from the heart - As we spend time in the heart of the labyrinth we now notice there are not one but two paths that lead to and away from the heart. Since we came in on the long path – the left path, we are now going to go out on what would be called the right path at the mouth of the labyrinth. However, when leaving the heart that same path is now on the left from our vantage point. Once this path is set upon we may notice that it feels very similar to a classic Cretan pattern. After 6 tight turns we find ourselves leaving the labyrinth next to the path we came in on.

Starting from the mouth – As we approach the mouth of the Aquarian Labyrinth, we notice two pathways before us. If we were to take the path on the right and follow it, we would find ourselves on a simple labyrinth that meanders and eventually deposits us at the Heart of the labyrinth. Not much different than walking a simple classic – Cretan Labyrinth. Except for one detail, this labyrinth is surrounded by a much larger labyrinth. Once at the heart, It is clear that the journey has not ended at the heart.

Chapter 10 – So, you want to build a Labyrinth...

After that first encounter with the labyrinth in Lilydale and meeting Sig, so many years ago. I left that workshop weekend with a new life goal in mind. I wanted to build a labyrinth of my own. At the time, I didn't have any property to put I non, and I didn't know anyone crazy enough to let me build on their property. That came later.

My point is, I understand the strong urge that the labyrinth can place on a person's mind or heart. I have heard it said, "Once someone starts to think about building a labyrinth. The spirit of the labyrinth will do everything it can to bring itself into reality." The way I have experienced labyrinths manifest, I tend to believe it.

It may seem strange to our 21st century American mind, the idea that a "thing" could have a spirit or a personality. In my experience, this is exactly what happens.

Creating Sacred Space

Labyrinths are sacred circles. Circles within circles, creating sacred space. For this reason, building a labyrinth should not be taken lightly. For, once you build it, you then have the responsibility of caring for it, protecting it, sharing it and loving it. These are things that some may not think about before building one. Creating the initial sacred space is important. But equally important is being a good steward of the labyrinth and respecting it. It doesn't matter if it's a classic and Aquarian or another contemporary design, Building a Labyrinth comes with responsibility.

Caring for the labyrinth does not end when you build it, it just begins. Caring for a labyrinth is more than just landscaping. It also includes walking it regularly, praying over it and talking to it. As I mentioned earlier, a labyrinth emulates or is a model of the pebble in the pond. This is why it is very important to be clear with your intentions in having and caring for a labyrinth.

Some things you may want to ask yourself before taking on the project are, Is this going to be a private space for just you? Or do you intend to share it with just close friends and family? Do you plan to have visitors? Will it be open to the public? What purpose do you wish to instill? Is it a peace or healing walk? Do you plan to dance it? Will it be used for prayer walks? Will you be doing rituals or ceremonies within the sacred circle? Will you use it to mark the solstices and equinoxes? This is a good time to have a clear idea of what you plan to do or accomplish in having a labyrinth.

The labyrinth that resides in my backyard, has experienced all of the above at different times in its existence. I mention these things here because you may have not thought about what it meant to be responsible for a sacred space. I just wanted to bring it to your awareness.

Please don't get me wrong. Caring for a labyrinth is a wonderful journey which can bring much inner growth. I just want to stress that this is not something to be taken lightly and unless you intend to spend time with the labyrinth in your care, you may consider being content with drawing or painting labyrinth for a while.

Drawing a labyrinth and tracing the path with your finger can be as effective as physically walking one. The better you are at visualizations or imagination the more effective it will be. Going back to the Pebble in the pond analogy, when we walk the labyrinth mindfully and we pray or use affirmations, be prepared for things in your life to move and change. The concentric rings of the labyrinth, seem to have a magnifying effect on whatever it is that you are praying about.

Therefore, it is also important to guard you thoughts and words in and around the labyrinth. Positive words and thoughts will amplify in a positive manner. However, negative words and thoughts will also be amplified. If you catch yourself thinking or speaking negatively, simply stop! Do your best to clear your mind of the thought in question and say, "I cancel that though, or those words, with love and peace." Then do your best to replace it with a positive thought or statement.

Another thing to know about having or caring for a labyrinth is, people will find you. Now that we have Google Earth in our lives. People tend to find labyrinths this way. If it shows up on Google Earth, be prepared for people to stop by your house or property, asking you about the labyrinth. Sometimes neighbors will look at you strangely, especially if you have labyrinth gathering at the full moon or any other Sabat.

I realize that many people don't have the property to put a labyrinth. That's okay, There are still other options, such as making a portable labyrinth. It can be made out of rope, or painted on a canvas. Let your imagination help and guide you. As you become more intimate with labyrinths in general, great ideas will come to you. Is a new labyrinth trying to become reality through you?

Aquarian Labyrinth - 6 Circuit, made from extra firewood.

I will give you an example of a labyrinth wanting to be born. In 2011 when the Aquarian Labyrinth patterns came to me, I had just moved and was in no way ready or prepared for what as in store. However, the labyrinth knew. I was new in town and only knew one person. Besides my husband. However, that one person was instrumental in putting me in touch with someone who would be the key to allowing this labyrinth to be birthed. Hi name was Pete, and he had just moved to town the same week we did. H also knew our friend and asked if my husband and I could help him move from his old house, way out in the country, to his new house, in town. The new house sat on 2.4 acres and was very flat and had a beautiful view of Konocti, the dormant volcano that is a main landmark in the this area. After Pete had moved in to his new home and starting to get settled, I asked him if I could put a labyrinth on his property. His response was interesting, "Well, I don't know what

that is, but it sound cool, sure, why not?!", and that
was that. The cosmic order for the birth of a new
labyrinth had been placed.

For the next month and a half, my husband and I
would go out daily to hunt for rocks suitable for the
labyrinth. We gathered rock from every place we
could find them. One of the great things about living
in a volcanic area is the great variety of rocks. I
know we live a Lake County, but if it wasn't for the
many lakes here, this would probably be called
Rock County.

We found so much obsidian, the entire outside wall
was made of just obsidian. This was the first
labyrinth I had laid out on my own, and it was big.
The labyrinth I had on paper was 14 circuits, 3
circuits larger than the Chartres. When I laid it out, I
did it organically. Meaning I used the seed pattern
and "grew" it from there. This resulted in the heart
being very small and the pathways being very
narrow. It was beautiful! When finished we
estimated that it required 176, 5 gallon buckets of
rocks. Pete donated a large crystal to the project
which we gladly placed at the center. We were all
amazed at how the light would hit it and create
different effects at different times of day. It was
especially amazing at sunset. It was blissful walking
the newly birthed labyrinth daily. It seed that daily it
would reveal a little more about itself with each new
walk. However, something was nagging at me

about how short or squashed the inner labyrinth seemed to be. Once I reworked the pattern, on paper, into a circle the inner labyrinth expanded to its full potential. This nagging would have to continue for about three years before I could do anything about it.

The other thing that started nagging in the back of my mind, was something I had overlooked before construction began. I was so excited about the idea that I got the green light to go forward with the project, that I forgot to dowse the site before starting. Dowsing is a way to read subtle earth energies, including underground water channels. So even though the labyrinth was built, I dowsed anyway. Once dowsed I found that the actual site for the heart should have been about six feet sound-west of where it presently stood. Needless to say I felt disappointed in my efforts. Although I had created this wonderful place of peace and reflection, I knew that it had to be redone.

When I expressed my dis-content to my husband and new friends, they just told me it was good enough. We all saw how much work it would take to completely redo it. So my discontentment, sat. Little did I know, at the time, that I would one day in the near future, buy that property from Pete. So my suggestion to you, is, PLAN before you start! Even to the point of waiting a full year, just to see what happens on your land during the various seasons of the year. Maybe your chosen spot floods out every winter, or other unforeseen weather anomalies which can change during the year. Will you need to bring in some fill dirt or gravel? Or would you prefer to keep it natural? Are you going to plant or partially plant it? If so you may need to run drip-lines to keep everything alive. Just remember, the clearer your vision of the finished result, the easier it will be to create that vision. Not just for the labyrinth, but for all of your plans in life. This is also a good time to tune into the labyrinth. To see what it has to say. Are you meditating with your vision in mind? Are you getting specific images? Draw it, write it out in detail. Really get an image of how you see it. Make it clear in your mind and heart and it will come to pass.

Weeds

One of the largest challenges of keeping a labyrinth is the weeds. This is where the question of, "How natural do you want it to be?" comes in. Personally I like the look and feel of a natural labyrinth as opposed to a paved labyrinth. For this reason I originally decided to hire goats to be my gardeners. Where I live we have star-thistle in profusion. After a little research, I found that Nigerian Dwarfs love Star-thistle because they are both from the same part of the world. This created a whole new set of problems, like having to put up extra fencing to keep them out of everything that I don't want them

to eat. The good thing about goats is that they don't
move the rocks around like the big silly horse does.
The bad part of having goats, is that they will eat
just about everything you want to keep, like flowers
and herbs. It's a give and take. It has been
suggested that sheep keep the grass down better
without eating all of the plants you want to keep,
however, I cannot confirm this.

*Cupcake and Chocolate Chip taking a break in the
labyrinth.*

If having a natural labyrinth doesn't appeal to you,
either, for the look of it or the continual upkeep, is
more than you would like to take on, then maybe
you would like something done in stonework
pathways. I've visited some beautiful labyrinths that
were done out of cement paver stones. Pathways
have deep gravel and some can be mowed
because the walls are made of brick that has been
recessed into the ground. Personally I like this idea
because the labyrinth can be mowed easily since

the stones are very flat and do not interfere with landscaping by having rocks everywhere.

I hope this was helpful and helping you to look at how you will take care of your labyrinth. No matter what pattern you decide to build, you will have to care for it. If it's not cared for you will not want to walk it.

I encourage you to think about your goals and dreams about being a labyrinth keeper. What do you wish to accomplish in having a labyrinth on your property? How will your life change? Do you have room in your life for this new dynamic? Do you plan to plant it, or keep it spars? The more you imagine down to the last detail, the easier it will be to bring your labyrinth creation into manifest reality.

Whatever you decide... I know it will be beautiful!

Chapter 11 – Care and Feeding of Your Labyrinth

Having a labyrinth on your property has much responsibility. I made a few points about this in the last chapter, however most of the what was covered was the thought process that goes into it, and the mechanics of having and keeping it on a physical level.

This chapter will speak to the mental or spiritual side of keeping of caring for a labyrinth. There is much satisfaction that comes from creating or building a labyrinth on your own property. There is nothing like the feeling of having such a beautiful and powerful sacred space available to you anytime you wish to visit. In my experience, there is great comfort in knowing you have a space set aside to commune with spirit. Yet can also be shared with those who appreciate and respect such place. The more time spent with the labyrinth privately, the more you may feel called to share it with your community. As someone caring for a labyrinth, it is very important to understand a few things that I will touch on here.

The first thing to understand is that no one owns a labyrinth. The labyrinth comes to the labyrinth keeper when the labyrinth keeper is ready and

makes themselves available to be a keeper.
Making yourself available to the possibility of caring
for a labyrinth will align you with the vibration of the
labyrinth. Therefore drawing it to you and into your
personal life. Possibly you will find a situation
where you are the designated labyrinth keeper.

The next thing to bring up about caring for a
labyrinth, is the idea of commitment. One reason I
talked in depth about the physical caring of it, in the
last chapter, is because I wanted to emphasis the
physical work involved in it's care. Not to
discourage you, on the contrary, it is my intention to
create within you a commitment, which is what it
takes to keep a labyrinth in walking condition year
round.

As a labyrinth keeper you may find times when the
labyrinth "speaks" to you in some way. The more
time you spend with it, the better and clearer that
communication will become. You may even have
times of dreaming about the labyrinth. This too can
be a form of communication.

When you live with a labyrinth, you may find
yourself drawn to it at times of stress or
contemplation. Go with it. As you walk it daily, it will
become clearer to you what type of work you can
accomplish with this tool.

Hosting labyrinth walks is one of the facets of being
a Labyrinth Keeper. I know Labyrinth Keepers who

make the commitment to host a monthly labyrinth gathering at the new or full moon. If that is too much of a commitment you could have gatherings at the solstice, or equinox's. All of these traditional gatherings are great, and you can commit to as many or few s you would like to. You could also start slow with a yearly walk, such as on World Labyrinth Day, and increase the frequency as you like. Nothing is set in stone and there are no rules. Just do what you heart and or spirit tell you.

You may be at a point where you are not ready to share it. Maybe you would like to spend some time alone with it, without adding the energies of others just yer. That is perfectly fine. A labyrinth keeper should create a degree of intimacy with the labyrinth being tended. Each one has a different energetic feel. There will be times when you may be sharing the labyrinth with others and they may have questions. Regarding how to solve a problem, or a certain way to meditate. And since you have spent quality time with the labyrinth in your care, you will then know how to guide them on their way to finding the answers they seek.

As you get to know the labyrinth, it will start to reveal secrets to you. Ask questions, go within of answers. Keep a journal of you labyrinth dialogue. Looking back on it from a future time, you will be glad you did. To journal such discoveries, and then to look back and read it , will give you even deeper in site.

Another aspect of being a Labyrinth Keeper is protection. Not everyone who wishes to visit the labyrinth will have pure intentions. Therefore it is your responsibility to weed out those who may bring some negative energies to the party. It may be intentional or unintentional, regardless, it is important that you not only protect the sacred space of the labyrinth but also to protect yourself and other visitors. Periodic clearings with prayer, chanting and or smudging can clear the energies and re-balance to a neutral energy space. This can be done after visitors have left and you are alone with the labyrinth.

Chapter 12 – Portable Labyrinths

Although I love the look and feel of permanent labyrinths, there is something altogether different in the feel of a portable labyrinth. As most permanent labyrinths are commonly made of rock and stone, portable labyrinths can be as simple as a rope laid out on the ground or as elaborate as a painted canvas with special alcoves painted to hold stones crystals and candles. It can be as simple or as complicated as the bearer would like.

The rope labyrinth I made at the Tahoe Renaissance Faire. Due to the stage in the background, we had to move it for the second weekend.

Please indulge me to tell you a story. Once upon a time, I was a fairy. I lived in the land of bubbles and I worked at small weekend Renaissance Faires around Northern California for several years. One particular show was at camp Richardson in South Lake Tahoe, CA. I had a bubble booth where I sold bubble wands and I was starting to bring more interesting things to show at the Faires that I worked. That show was a two week show, meaning we did a show on the weekend and had all week to camp and relax. I put together a rope labyrinth that I fastened to the ground with gutter spikes and fender washers which I disguised with silk flowers. When setting up the labyrinth, everything went alright except I noticed in a few places I had to adjust the placement of driving in the gutter spike because occasionally I would hit a rock. The labyrinth was a big success! However due to logistics and flow of the crowd traffic of the previous weekend I was required to move the labyrinth and my booth to a different location within the faire site. The new site was nice, however when I went to drive in the gutter spikes this time, I seemed to hit a rock every time! Needless to say I was frustrated! I laid on the ground, looked up into the sky and cried "Now what am I supposed to do?" As I lay there, I suddenly heard from somewhere deep inside, "There are rocks everywhere." I looked around with new eyes and I realized spirit had once again given me a message on how to proceed by changing my medium.

I went over to my friend, who worked security, because I knew she had a radio. I asked her if she could get some help from some of the volunteers. She asked me what I needed and explained it to her. Before I knew it, I had twelve people standing in front of me asking me what to do. I instructed them to gather as many rocks approximately, "the size of your head", that they could find and bring them and make a pile over here. Immediately we all went to work gathering rock from around the site to use in the effort. Once we had a what I estimated as a large enough pile, I laid out the seed pattern and the first circuit. Then instructed the first volunteer to start at a given point and end at another given point, following the curve of the first line. Then the second volunteer and so on. As the others saw what we were doing they joined in as if they knew what to do. Once the circuits were complete, I made the switchbacks and it was done. It took thirteen people one hour to complete including gathering rock. We all stood back in amazement and enjoyed the fruit of our labor by silently walking the labyrinth and then having a group hug. The end…

This was the fastest labyrinth I ever built - with a little help from my friends! 12 people - one hour!

Besides the fact that this is a good story to share, I hope you understand why I shared it. For one it shows how a labyrinth build can become a team building exercise. More importantly to teach the idea of being flexible with your thinking. Just because you have done it one way in the past, doesn't mean you can't change the way you do it. In this case changing the medium made it seem more permanent even though it was later taken apart when the show was over. The point is, be creative, think of a new way to make one. Build one in the forest from branches or twigs. Something that will simply go back to the earth after you leave it. Build one on the beach from seaweed and driftwood. The only limit is your imagination.

Aquarian Labyrinth - On a Santa Cruz beach - simply made with a stick found on the beach.

You may be asking, why would you want a portable labyrinth? What purpose does it serve? Many people have space for a dedicated labyrinth. However, many more people do not have space for a dedicated labyrinth. A portable labyrinth can be made small enough for a rug, that one person could walk alone, or it could be made large enough for group participation. It can be setup in a matter of minutes in a large living room, backyard, or park, and taken down in just a short time. Portable labyrinths are nice to offer at park fairs and community events.

This is my favorite portable labyrinth. It's made from rope lite and people love walking it for evening events.

At this writing, I have only used rope as portable labyrinths. However, I have plans to make a few canvas labyrinths. I am looking at ways to make it lightweight for transport. My favorite rope labyrinth is made of rope-light. Sometimes it's hard to find a source for electricity, so I have been known to bring my huge generator to events just to run it. It makes a lot of noise, I just tell people to think of it as white noise to help them meditate. This rope labyrinth is great to offer at the holidays during Christmas tree lighting events and the like. It's a good way to promote your home labyrinth if you have one and you want to invite people to visit or make people aware that there is a labyrinth in their area.

The beauty of a portable labyrinth is that you can set it up and when you are done with whatever you are using it for, it can be stored and brought out again with out too much hassle of setting it up. Plus, no weeding!

Wedding labyrinths can also be setup in this manner. One way to make a beautiful and festive rope labyrinth is to get not only rope, but silk flower garlands as well. Wire the garlands to the rope and lay it out in the labyrinth pattern of your choice. This could also be done with rope light for an added touch, especially for a sunset wedding. If the hall is large enough and/or the labyrinth small enough, this could also be done indoors. Sounds very romantic.

I love hearing what other people do with portable labyrinths, they truly have a magic all their own. One minute it's here and the next, it's gone.

If you would like more information on making a canvas labyrinth, I recommend Melissa Gayle West's book – Exploring the Labyrinth. She goes into great detail about setting up a labyrinth with a homemade compass.

Sunset at the Aquarian Labyrinth - A-Ho!

Chapter 13 – The Labyrinth as a Healing Tool

I have been working with this labyrinth for a few years now and I am still amazed at how two labyrinths can emerge from the same pattern and yet somehow occupy the same space. As this pattern and I have gotten to know each other, I have come to realize that this is a path of love. As I began walking, and working with the Aquarian Labyrinth Patterns, I could feel the energy build. An energy I can only describe as love.

As we hurl ourselves recklessly toward the Age of Aquarius – 2150, love shall be the norm. Labyrinths in general are paths of peace. Although peace is a byproduct of love, love is still the highest vibration so working from love will naturally bring peace. I have seen and walked several labyrinths that label themselves as, "the peace labyrinth". Do I dare label this pattern, "The Love Labyrinth"? My point is simply this. Just as this pattern has revealed itself to me, it has also revealed its purpose, and I believe that purpose is to walk and dance the sacred spiral of love.

This path of love doesn't just exist in the path of the labyrinth, but in the path of our lives. As we walk the Aquarian Labyrinth path, it is a good time to reflect on our life outside the labyrinth, to see how we are dancing our walk of love in the world.

How is your compassion level? What are you doing to show love to the people around you. Not only those closest to you like friends and family, but in the larger world such as your local community and beyond. Are you involved? Do you seek to find a niche in your community that you can fill to bring the most good to the most amount of people possible? Some of the simplest things can be done to impact your world in a big way! Don't be afraid to step out in LOVE!

I have heard it said, "He who dies with the most toys wins. But what is winning? Is "winning", being bogged down with trappings of modern life, or is winning being content in knowing you did the right thing in a tough situation, or spending time developing your true self. Twists and turns in life give us situations to master. As we master these situations we realize that the hardest situation to overcome in most cases is ourselves in this human condition and our own expectations of ourselves.

Love

Keep in mind that the Aquarian Labyrinth path is a path of love. In my experience every labyrinth path is a path of love. I have seen many "peace" labyrinths here and there, but it occurs to me that if you are to have peace you must first experience love. I have said several times in this writing that love is the most powerful force in the universe. It is love that will raise our vibration and bring us into the new age of Aquarius. I know I am not alone in this belief. When I first heard this said by teachers in my past, I didn't quite understand it. Mostly because I had no idea, at the time, what love really was. As I started exploring love and taking the time to truly understand or try to understand the mystery of love. I say this as if I were an expert on love, nothing could be further from the truth. How does that old song go?, "I've looked at love, from both sides now... loves illusions I recall, I really don't know love at all." My point is, do any of us really know what love is? In our limited perception, we try to experience love. We say we love, but what IS love?

I've heard it said and I believe that love is the highest vibration in the universe. We experience that vibration here on earth and in this existence, but it is very limited in comparison to the vastness of the source vibration of love. For love is all there is. The absence of love, is fear. When fear is present it diminishes the complete and pure vibration of love. This is why as humans we cannot experience love in its purest and highest vibrational form. Unfortunately humans are fearful. It seems to come naturally to us. Not to say that love does not come to us naturally. It's just that when we are fearful, we block or diminish the vibration of love. Because of the amount of people operating at a lower vibration, it brings the vibration of love down for all humans, as a collective, and therefore we do not experience love in its truest and purest form.

Heart = Forgiveness

The center or goal of a labyrinth is traditionally a place of reflection or meditation before continuing on the journey. This goal/heart is no different in that aspect.

The feeling I get from the Aquarian labyrinth, is that this heart is a place of forgiveness among other things. After all we just walked a path of love to get here. Sitting in the place of forgiveness, can sometimes be uncomfortable. However, it is important for us to forgive if we are to truly heal. When forgiveness is given, it is not a sign of weakness or a way of saying the other person is right, nor does it mean that we condone the other person's actions.

Forgiveness is for our sake. Forgiveness is allowing ourselves to just let it go and move on with our other important business, such as our life. Forgiveness is a way to put the past where it belongs, in the past. For it is from our own heart, that forgiveness flows, so should it be with the labyrinth.

Remember the pebble in the pond? Sitting in the heart of the labyrinth gives us a new vantage point. A place where we are able to look at the situation clearly. When we forgive the situations that brought us to this place of healing, we can then see our waves of forgiveness sweep over the earth and calm the trouble that has brewed in our hearts and minds for so long. This is a place of just being, of letting go and allowing healing to take place.

This is a good place to use a forgiveness exercise. Some of the best work on this subject are by Byron Katie. All of her information is online and can be downloaded for free. I highly recommend you look her up

Gratitude

This final portion of the journey just might be the most important part. Gratitude, gratitude helps us to understand the shift that just took place. When we are seeking healing one of the most important parts of creating a healing environment is to create an attitude of gratitude. Gratitude solidifies love and allows the changes within to become permanent.

As you walk this shorter portion of the path, start mentioning all the things that you are grateful for. This can be as simple as being thankful for your breath.

I hope this is helpful to get you started, and maybe it will inspire you to come up with another way to

uoe the Aquarian Labyrinth as a healing tool. Listen
to your inner voice from the heart.

Chapter 14 – Dedication and Other Ceremonies

Dowsing the Site

It is very important to dowse the potential site BEFORE setting down stones. I strongly recommend you do this very important step. Every labyrinth I have ever setup has been dowsed and we have asked permission of the guardian spirits to place the labyrinth In a specific place. I have only been told No, once.

I will not go into dowsing here, even though I am an experienced dowser I don't feel I would do the subject justice. The place I have found to learn about dowsing has been from Sig Longren. He is the first teacher ever had on dowsing, and he is a world renowned expert. He has written several books on dowsing and labyrinths. If you don't want to learn how to dowse or if you just don't feel confident enough, there are dowsers aplenty if you look around in your local spiritual community. Whether you decide to do it yourself or not I recommend that you do a small ceremony to invoke the directions then engage the area guardians in whichever way you feel is appropriate and respectful.

Groundbreaking - Ceremony

We ask that the Spirit of the Divine creator who works through us, to look upon this project with blessings, guidance and love.

We also ask that the local guardian spirits who are agents of the divine creator be here to support, advise and protect us during this project.

We especially ask that the spirit of our earth mother be present and bless the materials that are being used as they came from her.

We promise to use this gift for the highest good of all involved.

We ask protection of this sacred space now in the future of its existence.

We ask that people working on this project, do so without injury or personal conflict.

We ask that all who experience this labyrinth be touched for their highest good

A-Ho!

Dedication

We are thankful for the opportunity to create this labyrinth, and we now bless it by the power of the Divine Creator who works through us.

We call upon the guardian spirits of the true light within this place to be present and to be a witness to this dedication.

We now surround this labyrinth with a bubble of divine white light, filled with love, healing and protection.

May all who walk this labyrinth; allow their hearts to be filled with unconditional love, and be healed according to their highest good. May the energies of this labyrinth always be pure and of the one light which is love.

If anyone walking this labyrinth releases energies which are not of the one light. May those energies be transformed into the divine light of love.

May the experiences of all who walk this labyrinth be for their highest good.

So be it! A-Ho!

New Year Labyrinth Ritual

A new year is often a time of reflection. Take this time to reflect on the year. This is best done IN a quiet relaxed state. You could even make your reflection a meditation on its own.

Some of the things to reflect on are:

- Job or housing changes

- Family relationships

- Family or personal finances

- Spiritual

Think about the following questions in regard to each subject.

- How do you feel about it/them

- Are you where you want to be?

- How do you desire to improve it/your relationship?

As you walk the labyrinth think on those things and let your mind wander as your feet wander. Remember, there is no wrong way to walk the labyrinth, walk it and think as you wish. You may be surprised of the outcome.

Labyrinth Blessing Ritual

Purpose:

To bless the labyrinth for future spiritual use.

Tools Needed:

Stick of incense (Smudge Stick if available)

Small candle

Cup of water

Dish of Earth or Salt

Four participants that wish to participate in the ritual. To have four people who represent the four elements according to their astrological sign gives the ritual that much more power.

By the power of the divine creator that works through us.

We cleanse and consecrate these elemental symbols. With the intention of cleansing and consecrating this labyrinth to define it as a sacred space.

1. First   person takes the incense and walks to the opening of the labyrinth and says: "By the power of the Divine Creator, I cleanse and consecrate this labyrinth and define this as a sacred space by the power of Air."

    They then walk the labyrinth.

2. Second person takes the candle , walks to the opening of the labyrinth and says: "By the power of the Divine Creator, I cleanse and consecrate this labyrinth and define this as a sacred space by the power of Fire." They should then walk the labyrinth carrying the candle, imagining the candle fire is cleansing the labyrinth space as they walk.

3. Third person takes the vessel of water, walks to the opening of the labyrinth and says: "By the power of the Divine Creator, I cleanse and consecrate this labyrinth and define this as a sacred space by the power of Water." They should then walk the labyrinth while using a small branch with leaves to sprinkle

the water as they go.

4. Fourth person takes the earth/salt and
    walks to the opening of the   labyrinth and
    says: "By the power of the Divine Creator, I
    cleanse and consecrate this labyrinth and
    define this as a sacred space by the power
    of Earth. "
    They then walk the labyrinth while sprinkling
    the earth/salt.

5. Fifth person walks to the opening of the
    labyrinth and says: "In the   name of the
    spirit of the Divine Creator I cleanse,
    consecrate and bless this Labyrinth, and
    define it as a sacred space by the power of
    the light of spirit.

    So Be it!

When all have reached the center of the labyrinth
the elements are left in the center. The incense and
candles are left to burn out, the water and salt are
poured out onto the earth or onto rocks.

Chapter 15 - Labyrinths & Weddings

An aspect of the Aquarian Labyrinth I have discovered is it's capacity of lending itself to wedding ceremonies, both large and small. I'm sure that one reason this aspect appeals to me, is because among other things I am a wedding officiant.

I have seen weddings that incorporate a classic labyrinth pattern. However the flow never seemed right to me, because no matter if the bride walked it by herself or the bride and groom walk it together, at the end it seem as little convoluted. I have even seen them just step over the border to get out instead of walking back through the labyrinth. My experience with the Aquarian Labyrinth, is that it flows.

I will not go into ceremonial details here. This chapter can be used as a basic model and the details of the ceremony can be added to the taste of the couple being joined.

The Aquarian Labyrinth allows for small intimate weddings to include the guest walk the labyrinth, following the wedding party. This means that the guests will be standing for the duration of the ceremony. So this could be done closer to the end. Chairs can be placed just outside the labyrinth for those who are not physically able to walk it or do not wish to walk the entire labyrinth. Having the guests walk as well brings them into the ceremony and surrounds the couple with love from all their friends and family.

As the ceremony concludes, the couple can have the receiving line in the heart of the labyrinth. The officiate should bring up any elders who may have not walked and are sitting, to come into the heart by walking up the path on the right and stepping over the barrier to congratulate the couple. Once the elders go, then they may just sit back down while all the others go through the receiving line, past the bride and groom and out the shorter path. Since in this manner the bride and groom leave the heart last, a decorated broom can be placed at the mouth of the path for them to jump over, optional of course.

The above idea was laid out using the Aquarian Labyrinth 6 circuit. If you look below you will see the Aquarian Wedding Labyrinth. This labyrinth lends itself to an entirely different experience. Notice how the two labyrinths are side by side and mirror each other. A representation of how as a couple we mirror each other. As the couple approach the officiate the separate paths of the two labyrinths are apparent Traditionally the groom on

the right and the bride on the left each would walk
the path in front of them.

If this is an LGBT wedding they would pick ahead
of time which side they stand on, according to
feeling rather than tradition, and naturally which
path they will be walking during the ceremony.

The officiate can start the wedding by bringing the
couple to the altar at the opening of the labyrinths.
Here the officiate can say a few words. One thing
they might talk about is how the separate labyrinths
represent the couple walking their life path before
coming together.

Walking the entry path

The couple should reflect on that aspect of their lives as they walk. As the couple walk, this is a good time to have someone play a song, read a poem, etc.

Pausing at the Heart

Pausing at the heart for individual reflection. Vows or pledges can be made from the place of the labyrinth heart.

Walking the exit path

As the couple leave the heart and walk out on the shorter path, it is time to project to the future a lifetime of love and partnership. At this time the guests should also be sending loving thoughts to the couple regarding their future life together.

Upon exiting this shorter path the couple will be facing each other and the officiate will be facing the audience. Here the final vows will be taken and they will walk out on the path where two become one.

Chapter 16 – Wilbur

In real life, I am a California Certified Massage Therapist. In May of 2017, I started working at Wilbur Hot Springs in Williams CA, just a hop skip and jump over the from me in Clearlake. Not too long after starting I found out that they had been talking about putting in a labyrinth. One part of what we call the Wilbur experience is the hot springs, like they say, "In all the world, no waters like these". It's true! Wilbur possesses wonderfully healing sulfur baths.

The other part of the Wilbur experience is the 1,300 acre nature preserve. The area is rugged, rocky and beautiful, and although it seems pristine on the surface, it doesn't take long to realize people have been here a long time. The area used to be a quicksilver mine town and the hot springs is what made it bearable I'm sure. You had to be rough and tough to survive out here. The baths were founded in 1865 and there is a whole history which goes along with the place.

After approaching management with the idea that I could build it for them and giving them a choice of a traditional pattern or the Aquarian, they said yes and chose the Aquarian 6. The next day we took a ride out to the preserve to find a suitable location. I knew as soon as I saw it. A beautiful mostly flat area near the creek and one lone oak tree. As soon as I saw it, I was compelled. I walked over to the tree and looked at the beauty of it's branches as they created an umbrella over the surrounding area around its trunk.. Then I remembered seeing this site in a dream a few years ago. It was perfect!

The first day I went out to the site by myself to start work early in the morning, sunup, and it was mid June. As I approached the site I could hear buzzing. Not too far from the site are bee boxes so I didn't think anything of it. Once I got under the canopy of the tree, the buzzing was more intense. I looked at the ends of the lower branches and saw two or three bees on each of the acorn buds coming out on the tips of the branches. As I walked to the trunk I could actually feel the buzzing in my body. I sat the trunk of the tree and meditated on the beauty I found around me. I gave thanks to the tree and asked permission to build this sacred site at it's base. At this point the buzzing got louder and my emotions were overflowing through my heart. I felt love flowing from the earth energy around me and I felt grateful that I was here to experience it. I connected with the tree and the bees. I accepted their blessing and so the work began.

Since it was already mid-June when I stared, and this part of Nor-Cal gets quite hot in the summer, I took the one mile walk early in the morning and many times arrived at the build site just as the sun was coming over the hill. Most days I could only work an hour or two before it was too hot. I continued working on it when I was there. At that point I was there two to three times a month for several days in a row. Working on it in this manner took about three months to complete. The maintenance manager kept a close eye on the project and was quick to bring more piles of rocks for me to work with.

Through all the hard work of making the Aquarian Labyrinth happen at Wilbur, I have through it all felt blessed. To have not been there very long, yet trusted with a long term change of the landscape. I feel both guided and blessed. I expect to remain a part of Wilbur, always!

Blessed Be!

The Gates of Wilbur - Founded 1965

The Beginnings of something great! After finishing the first 3 circles, I realized that I needed more room in the center. So I removed the stones in the center to open up the inner pathway.

Finishing up the outside circle. Almost done!

The finished product as it looked a few months after finishing it. It took about one month of working on it early in the morning before work and before it got too hot.

This sign was erected by Wilber. I was surprised when they put my name on it. I am deeply honored that they allowed me to bring the Aquarian Labyrinth to be part of the landscape at Wilbur.

Looking at the finished labyrinth from a distance. It invites you to come walk it's paths and discover its secrets.

Bibliography & Suggested Reading

- Sig Lonegren -
  - Labyrinths: Ancient Myths and Modern Uses
  - The Pendulum Kit
  - Spiritual Dowsing: Tools for Exploring the Intangible Realms
  - Sacred Space Handbook
  - Memoirs of a Geomancer: On Gnowing, Rational or Irrational? No, both!

- Lauren Artress -
  - Walking the Sacred Path: Rediscovering the Labyrinth as a Spiritual Practice

- Helen Raphael Sands -
  - The Healing Labyrinth

- Malissa Gayle West -
  - Exploring the Labyrinth: A Guide for Healing and Spiritual Growth